Employment Law and the European Convention on Human Rights

Bulletin of Comparative Labour Relations

VOLUME 114

Founding Editor

The series started in 1970 under the dynamic editorship of Professor Roger Blanpain (Belgium), former President of the International Industrial Relations Association. Professor Blanpain, Professor Emeritus of Labour Law, Universities of Leuven and Tilburg, was also General Editor of the International Encyclopedia of Laws (with more than 1,600 collaborators worldwide) and President of the Association of Educative and Scientific Authors Authors. He passed away in October 2016.

General Editor

In 2015 Frank Hendrickx, Professor of labour law at the Faculty of Law of the University of Leuven (Belgium) joined as a co-Editor. Frank Hendrickx has published numerous articles and books and regularly advises governments, international institutions and private organisations in the area of labour law as well as in sports law. He is the Editor-in-Chief of the European Labour Law Journal and General Editor of the International Encyclopaedia of Laws.

Introduction

The Bulletins constitute a unique source of information and thought-provoking discussion, laying the groundwork for studies of employment relations in the 21st century, involving among much else the effects of globalization, new technologies, migration, and the greying of the population.

Contents/Subjects

Amongst other subjects the Bulletins frequently include the proceedings of international or regional conferences; reports from comparative projects devoted to salient issues in industrial relations, human resources management, and/or labour law; and specific issues underlying the multicultural aspects of our industrial societies.

Objective

The Bulletins offer a platform of expression and discussion on labour relations to scholars and practitioners worldwide, often featuring special guest editors.

The titles published in this series are listed at the end of this volume.

Employment Law and the European Convention on Human Rights

The Research of the Recent Jurisprudence of the ECtHR Related to Employment Law (2017-2021)

Elena Sychenko & Adalberto Perulli*

General Editor
Frank Hendrickx

Founding Editor
Roger Blanpain

Wolters Kluwer

* Chapters 1-5 are written by Elena Sychenko. Chapters 6-8 are written by Adalberto Perulli.

Published by:
Kluwer Law International B.V.
PO Box 316
2400 AH Alphen aan den Rijn
The Netherlands
E-mail: lrs-sales@wolterskluwer.com
Website: www.wolterskluwer.com/en/solutions/kluwerlawinternational

Sold and distributed by:
Wolters Kluwer Legal & Regulatory U.S.
920 Links Avenue
Landisville, PA 17538
United States of America
E-mail: customer.service@wolterskluwer.com

Printed on acid-free paper.

ISBN 978-94-035-3556-2

e-Book: ISBN 978-94-035-4066-5
web-PDF: ISBN 978-94-035-4076-4

Printed in the Netherlands.

Notes on Authors

Adalberto Perulli, full professor of labour law, Ca Foscari University of Venice.

Since 2000 he has been an invited professor at the Paris Nanterre University, where he teaches, in French, as part of the Doctoral and Master's degree courses in Droit Social. He is the director of the GESAM Master and the Master in Human Rights and Democratization of the European Inter-University Center (EIUC). He has published numerous works on labour law and industrial relations. He has done research for the European Commission and for the ILO.

Elena Sychenko, PhD, associate professor, Saint Petersburg University; adjunct professor, University of Bologna.

She received her PhD from the University of Catania in 2016, and a Master's with honours from Saint Petersburg State University in 2004. She is the academic director of the Master's program Transnational legal practice at Saint Petersburg State University. She was ILO external consultant in the projects 'Country study on preventing and addressing violence and harassment through OSH framework in El Salvador' (November 2022-February 2023) and 'Situation and Gap Analysis Report on Forced Labour Protocol - PAKISTAN' (2020-2021). She is a Certified trainer for HELP online courses, Council of Europe, and trainer of the HELP course 'Labour rights as human rights'. She received an Erasmus + Jean Monnet Module 'European Labour Law' (2019-2022).

Table of Contents

Introduction

In the last two decades, there has been a significant move towards recognizing the fundamental nature of labour rights through the so-called constitutionalization of labour rights[1] and researching the 'labour facets' of international human rights treaties.[2] The present research follows this trend. In 2016, the research on the relevance of the European Convention on Human Rights (ECHR) to the protection of individual labour rights was published by Wolters Kluwer; it provided the concept of integration of labour rights, researched the history of the ECHR and analysed cases which were considered by the European Court of Human Rights (ECtHR) till 2016.[3] The present book is to be seen as a second volume, as those topics which were part of the first book will not be repeated here, but are still needed to understand the evolution of the approach of the ECtHR to labour law cases. Under labour law cases, we understand the applications of the protection of labour rights (right to collective bargaining, to strike, to wage) and of human rights at work (workplace privacy, freedom of religion at work, etc.).

---

1. J. Fudge, 'Constitutionalizing Labour Rights in Europe', in: T. Campbell, K. Ewing and A. Tompkins (eds) *The Legal Protection of Human Rights: Sceptical Essays*. Oxford University Press, 2011, 244-267. Available at SSRN, https://ssrn.com/abstract=1551587; R. Dukes, 'Constitutionalizing Employment Relations: Sinzheimer, Kahn-Freund, and the Role of Labour Law'. *Journal of Law and Society* 35:3 (2008): 341-363; D. Gagne and M-J. Dupuis, 'Constitutionnalisation du Droit du Travail et Transformation du Devoir de Representation Sindicale: Quelques Questionnements Concernant les Clauses Orphelin'. *Canadian Labour and Employment Law Journal* 20 (2017): 1.
2. N. Bruun, L. Klaus, S. Isabelle and C. Stefan (eds) *The European Social Charter and the Employment Relation*. Hart Publishing. Oxford 2017; F. Dorssemont and K. Lörcher, *The European Convention on Human Rights and the Employment Relation*. Hart Publishing, 2013; V. Mantouvalou, 'Labour Rights in the European Convention on Human Rights: An Intellectual Justification for an Integrated Approach to Interpretation'. *Human Rights Law Review* 13:3 (2013): 529-555; B. Likić-Brborić, and S. Carl-Ulrik, 'Labour Rights as Human Rights? Trajectories in the Global Governance of Migration'. *Migration, Precarity, & Global Governance: Challenges and Opportunities for Labour. Oxford University Press* (2015): 223-244.
3. E. Sychenko, 'Individual Labour Rights as Human Rights: The Contributions of the European Court of Human Rights to Worker's Rights Protection', Roger Blanpain, Frank Hendrickx (eds). *Wolters Kluwer International. Bulletin of Comparative Labour Relations*, Vol. 96. 2017, 268 p.

This research is based on more than fifty related employment law cases considered by the ECtHR in the period 2017-2021. It traces the development of legal positions of the Court in the sphere of individual and collective rights and the realization of human rights at work, such as an employee's privacy, freedoms of religion and expression. It also considers the development of the approach of the ECtHR to forced labour and human trafficking and underlines the value of the International Labour Organization standards for the court's reasoning. The book focuses on the recent trends of the ECHR's case law, such as human rights in the COVID era and the consideration of cases on unfair dismissal in light of the ECHR.

Our key objective is to demonstrate the actual applicability of ECHR for the protection of labour rights and human rights at work, to raise awareness of national lawyers about the possibility of referring to the norms of the Convention and its jurisprudence in national proceedings and, finally, bringing the case to Strasbourg, if all national remedies are exhausted. The violation of labour rights listed in the ECHR, for example, of the freedom of association (Article 11), the prohibition of forced labour (Article 4), or discrimination in employment (Protocol 12) might be considered a violation of the negative obligations of the states under ECHR, if the applicant was employed by the State or the violation is attributable to the State. Also, private employees might bring a case before the ECtHR if the states did not ensure due protection of these rights in domestic proceedings as they have positive obligations to secure the rights under ECHR to those within their jurisdiction.[4] The same might be said about those labour rights which are not directly mentioned in the ECHR but were integrated into it through the broad interpretation of the ECtHR (the right to strike and collective bargaining (Article 11), and about human rights at work. The latter also can be either explicitly mentioned in the text of the Convention (e.g., freedom of expression (Article 10)) or deduced from its text (the right to develop relations with others (Court's interpretation of Article 8).

This book has academic value as well: the significant broadening of the scope of Article 8 protecting the right to private life will be one of the key points of the research. The judges of the court have recently noted that 'almost any situation of dismissal from work will trigger the applicability of Article 8, transforming a large number of labour law disputes into litigation for the protection of private life'.[5] It is very important for both human rights doctrine and the purpose of protection of labour rights to try to determine the possible borders of application of Article 8 in cases of unfair dismissal or other violations of the right to work.

The structure of the book follows the idea of the authors to consider the approach of the Court to the protection of individual and collective labour rights: first, we will briefly explain the reasons and the methods of the integration of labour rights in the ECHR. In the absence of the definitions of rights in the ECHR, the reference of the Court to other international treaties has become one of the key legal methods for considering

4. ECtHR, Eweida and Others v. The United Kingdom (48420/10 36516/10 51671/10) 15/01/2013, para. 83.
5. Dissenting opinion of the judges Wojtyczek, Polačkova and Ktistakis to the majority judgment in the case Budimir v. Croatia (App No. 44691/14) 16/12/2021.

'labour law' cases. This is why, in the first chapter, the value of ILO standards for the ECtHR's decision-making will be researched. The second chapter is dedicated to the case law on individual labour rights and human rights at work, such as the Prohibition of Slavery, Servitude, Forced or Compulsory Labour, Discrimination, the right to respect for private life and freedom of thought, religion and expression at work. The last part will consider the recent jurisprudence on the protection of collective labour rights.

CHAPTER 1

The Integration of Labour Rights in the ECHR and the Value of ILO Standards

The ECHR was the first supranational instrument recognizing the human rights of people, adopted sixteen years before the International Human Rights Covenants at the level of the UN. The European Convention focused on civil and political rights, creating an efficient system of defending the post-war European democracy of Western Europe. However, already during the drafting period of the Convention in the forties of the XX century, there were ideas to create a 'complete code of all the freedoms and fundamental rights, and all the so-called social freedoms and rights'.[6] They were not heard though. One of the fathers of the Convention, Sir David Maxwell-Fyfe, pointed out that these rights were 'too controversial and difficult to enforce even in the changing state of social and international development in Europe'. In his view, their inclusion could jeopardize the wider acceptance of the ECHR.[7]

Thus, social rights remained, in 1950, out of the system of the ECHR and were explicitly recognized in the legal order of the Council of Europe only with the adoption of the European Social Charter (ESC) in 1964. The reference to the system of the ESC is needed in the context of this chapter as ECHR and the ESC are often seen as the two counterparts of the human rights regime of the Council of Europe (CoE). Comparing them might be helpful for understanding the reasons for the integration of labour rights into the scope of the ECHR.[8]

6. These are words said by Pierre-Henri Teitgen while presenting the Draft of the ECHR on 19 August 1949, cited from E. Bates, (ed.) *The Evolution of the European Convention on Human Rights: From Its Inception to the Creation of a Permanent Court of Human Rights*. Oxford University Press, New York 2010, 59.
7. *See* Collected Edition of the 'Travaux Préparatoires' of the European ECHR on Human Rights: Preparatory Commission of the Council of Europe, Committee of Ministers, Consultative Assembly, 11 May-8 September 1949. Council of Europe. BRILL, 1975, p. 116.
8. *See*, e.g., C. O'Cinneíde, 'The European Social Charter and EU Labour Law'. Alan Bogg, Cathryn Costello, and A. C.L. Davies, *Research Handbook on EU Labour Law*. Edward Elgar Publishing, 2016, 191-214.

ESC included a large set of labour rights, both individual and collective. However, due to the peculiarities of the monitoring system, the efficiency of protecting those rights under the Charter always left much to be desired. In contrast with the system of the ECHR, the Charter did not provide the possibility of making an individual complaint/application in case of the violation of rights but only the classical way of monitoring compliance through the consideration of the States' reports. The envisaged system of collective complaints is only an additional method. Collective complaints under the ESC might be brought against those states which have ratified an additional protocol, adopted by the Council of Europe in 1995. But even if the country has ratified this protocol, there are no clear norms in the Charter to establish the binding legal character of the conclusions of the European Committee of Social Rights that considers both the collective complaints and the state's reports.

The system of the ECHR provides an opportunity for an individual complaint in case of the violation of human rights; the judgments of the ECtHR are binding and might lead to the reopening of the judicial proceedings in the Member State and the reconsideration of the case.[9] Therefore, the system of the ECHR provides a much more efficient mechanism of protection and has a long story of successful impact on the legislation and the jurisprudence of the CoE Member States.[10] Appreciating the efforts of the CoE in implementing the ESC and the hard work of the European Committee of Social Rights, it is needless to say that the results of this work are more moderate because of the peculiarities of the system adopted by the Member States.

Presumably, being aware of this disparity and being faced with the neo-liberal attacks on social rights, the ECtHR starts to integrate the possibility of protection of certain social and labour rights under the Convention. Already in the 1970s, the Court stated that there was no 'water-tight division' separating economic and social rights from the field covered by the ECHR[11] and that the 'living interpretation'[12] of the ECHR is needed. The Court's perception of human rights as indivisible and the aspiration to ensure that the norms do correspond to the actual societal needs made the Court interpret certain articles much broader than before. In the opinion of Alessandra Di Martino, ECtHR's increasing resort to an 'evolutive construction' of the Convention, adapting it to changing and shared social needs, can be read as a compensation for the lack of a legislator in Strasbourg.[13] This approach permitted to include the new rights

9. Recommendation R (2000)2 of the Committee of Ministers to Member States on the re-examination or Reopening of Certain Cases at Domestic Level Following Judgments of the Court, adopted on 19 January 2000.
10. *See* an interactive site dedicated to tracing the impact of the ECtHR on Member States: CoE. Impact of the ECHR. https://www.coe.int/en/web/impact-convention-human-rights#/.
11. ECtHR, Airey v. Ireland (6289/73) 9 October 1979, para. 26.
12. ECtHR, Tyrer v. The United Kingdom (5856/72) 25 April 1978, para. 31. *See also*: G. Letsas 2013. 'The ECHR as a Living Instrument: Its Meaning and its Legitimacy'. In *The European Court of Human Rights in a National, European and Global Context*, ed. G. Ulfstein, A. Føllesdal, and B. Peters, 106–141. Cambridge: Cambridge University Press. Available at SSRN, http://ssrn.com/abstract=2021836 (accessed 20 September 2014).
13. A. Di Martino, 'National Constitutions and the ECHR', in: G. Repetto (ed.) *The Constitutional Relevance of the ECHR in Domestic and European Law. An Italian Perspective.* Intersentia Cambridge. Portland 2013, 133.

to the scope of ECHR (e.g., the right to collective bargaining,[14] the right to strike,[15] or the right to wage[16]) and to recognize the particular value of certain rights at work (workplace privacy,[17] for example, or occupational health[18]). The examples of such integration will be considered below.

1.1 INDIVISIBILITY OF HUMAN RIGHTS AND THEIR LIVING INTERPRETATION BY THE ECtHR

The Vienna Declaration and Programme of Action, adopted at the World Conference on Human Rights in June 1993, proclaims solemnly: 'The international community must treat human rights globally in a fair and equal manner, on the same footing, and with the same emphasis.'[19] The European Court explicitly emphasized the indivisibility of human rights already in 1979. In the Airey v. Ireland judgment, the Court noted the following: 'The mere fact that an interpretation of the Convention may extend into the sphere of social and economic rights should not be a decisive factor against such an interpretation; there is no water-tight division separating that sphere from the field covered by the Convention.'[20]

It has become possible through the reference to other international treaties and to the comparative research of the laws and jurisprudence of the state members in the field of labour rights, establishing a so-called European consensus. The process of finding a European consensus might be understood as detecting through a comparative research a sample of a legal approach (regulations or case law) accepted by a number of European states, which permit a certain level of protection of a social right. As an example, we can refer to the establishment of the right of fathers to receive paternity benefits[21] or paternity leaves in the case law of the ECtHR.[22]

Integration by the Court of new rights into the scope of the Convention occurs, as a rule, after the establishment of a consensus among European states regarding the protection of a particular right. For example, in the landmark case on discrimination (Konstantin Markin v. Russia), the Court found a violation of Articles 8 and 14 of the ECHR, establishing that most European countries, unlike Russia, grant male military servants the right to parental leave. Thus, the Court included the right to parental leave within the protective scope of the Convention by broadly interpreting the right to respect for family life, affirming the principle of the indivisibility of human rights in practice.

14. Demir and Baykara v. Turkey (34503/97) 12 November 2008.
15. Ognevenko v. Russia, n. 44873/09, § 73, 20 November 2018.
16. ECtHR, Smokovitis and others v. Greece (46356/99) 11 April 2002.
17. López Ribalda and Others v. Spain ([GC] 1874/13 8567/13) 17 November 2019.
18. Meier v. Switzerland (10109/14) 9 February 2016.
19. Vienna Declaration and Programme of Action, adopted by the World Conference on Human Rights in Vienna on 25 June 1993. Available at, http://www.ohchr.org/en/professionalinterest/pages/vienna.aspx (accessed 20 November 2014).
20. ECtHR, Airey v. Ireland (6289/73) 09/10/1979, para. 26.
21. Petrovic v. Austria (20458/92) 27 March 1998.
22. Markin Konstantin v. Russia (No. 30078/06) Grand Chamber, 22 March 2012.

Such an approach raises many questions and is often severely criticized by scholars, judges and, definitely, Member States. The said judgment in Markin v. Russia has become the first stumbling block to disturb the relations between the ECtHR and the Russian Constitutional Court.[23] The president of the Russian Constitutional Court stated that establishing European consensus is inconsistent with the basic principles of the ECHR.[24] Also, the judge of the ECtHR noted that the European Court has jurisdiction to apply the convention, and not to edit it, and only the parties to the Convention can change the content of their obligations.[25] Former Judge Franz Matscher argued that the ECtHR has reached the limits of interpretation of the text of the Convention and sometimes goes beyond these limits, intruding into the realm of legal policy.[26]

Despite criticism, the 'living' approach to the convention has become characteristic of the ECtHR. Today it is generally recognized that the interpretation of the Convention is a dynamic process that takes place 'in the light of changing values in European societies and new challenges in the field of human rights protection caused by advances in areas of science and technology that could not have been imagined back in 1950'.[27] Largely due to the dynamic approach to defining the rights protected by the Convention, labour and social security rights have come to the attention of the ECtHR, and the European Convention, given the growing authority and scope of the rights covered, has acquired 'a truly constitutional character for the entire European continent'.[28]

To provide an example of the integration of new rights to the scope of the ECHR, the expansion of the interpretation of Articles 3 and 8 of the ECHR will be considered as most illustrative.

1.1.1 Interpretation of the Prohibition of Torture (Article 3 of the ECtHR) and Social Rights

According to Article 3 ECHR, no one shall be subjected to torture or to inhuman or degrading treatment or punishment. The article was aimed at protecting the security of people. It is clear from the preparatory works to Article 3 that only physical safety was

23. V. Zorkin, *The Limits of Pliability* (Predel ustupchivosti) Rossyskaya gazeta, Vol. 5325 Issue 246, 29 October 2010.
24. V. Zorkin, 'Problems of Implementation of the Human Rights Convention'. *Journal of Foreign Law and Comparative Law* 5:54 (2015): 812-819. doi:10.12737/16128.
25. Partly dissenting opinion of judge Pinheiro Farinha in Marckx v. Belgium (6833/74) 06/13/1979, para. 4.
26. F. Judge Matscher, 'Methods of Interpretation of the Convention', in: R.St. J. Macdonald et al. (eds) *The European System for the Protection of Human Rights*, Martinus Nijhoff Publishers, 1993, 69-70.
27. M. Pellonpaa, 'Continuity and Change in the Case-Law of the European Court of Human Rights', in: La Promotion de la Justice, Des Droits de L'homme Et Du Règlement Des Conflits Par Le Droit International edited by Marcelo Gustavo Kohen. Martinus Nijhoff Publishers, 2007, 409.
28. P. Mahoney, ' The European Convention on Royal Rights: Royalty, Aristocracy and The European Convention on Human Rights', in: La Promotion de la Justice, *Des Droits de L'homme Et Du Règlement Des Conflits Par Le Droit International edited by Marcelo Gustavo Kohen.* Martinus Nijhoff Publishers, 2007. 341.

in the minds of the drafters.[29] However, half a century later, the prohibition of degrading treatment was interpreted by the court as being also related to the sphere of realization of social rights of citizens. In particular, in MSS v. Belgium and Greece,[30] the Court recognized that extreme poverty may, in some cases, amount to degrading treatment.[31] The court found a violation by Greece of Article 3 ECHR, since an emigrant deported to Greece spent months living in poverty, unable to meet his basic needs - food, hygiene and shelter - in fear of being attacked and robbed. The same conclusion was later reached in N.H. and Others v. France, where five men seeking asylum in France were forced to sleep rough in the street for several months incapable to meet their basic subsistence needs.[32] The Court explained that it cannot exclude the possibility of State responsibility under Article 3 for 'treatment' where an applicant, in circumstances wholly dependent on State support, 'finds himself or herself faced with official indifference when in a situation of serious deprivation or want incompatible with human dignity'.[33] This approach is far beyond the initial will of the states to ensure the physical security of persons.

In other decisions, the Court indicated the possibility of considering cases of insufficient pensions as violating the prohibition of degrading treatment. In two judgments against Russia, the ECtHR noted that in order to prove a violation of Article 3 ECHR, an applicant receiving a severely inadequate pension must prove that the degrading treatment was of a certain severity (minimum level of severity). This threshold is considered to have been reached when the ill-treatment involves bodily injury or severe physical or mental suffering or degrades the individual by demonstrating a lack of respect for his human dignity.[34] In these two cases against Russia (Lareshina v. Russia and Budina v. Russia), the ECtHR decided that the applicants had not substantiated their allegations that the lack of money caused them specific suffering,[35] even though the level of their pensions was much below the living wage in Russia and absolutely insufficient for survival.

Despite the refusal to consider the applications of Russian pensioners on the merits, the very possibility of presenting applications that the pension is insufficient as degrading recipients, which was recognized by the Court in these decisions, is already a significant step forward. The scholars note that this conclusion of the Court can be of great importance for expanding the scope of protection of social rights of the ECHR.[36]

29. European Commission of Human Rights. Preparatory works on Article 3 of the ECHR. 22 May 1956. Available at, https://www.echr.coe.int/LibraryDocs/Travaux/ECHRTravaux-ART3-DH(56)5-EN1674940.pdf.
30. ECtHR, MSS v. Belgium and Greece (30696/09) Grand Chamber 21/01/2011; *See* G. Clayton, 'Asylum Seekers in Europe: MSS v. Belgium and Greece'. *Human Rights Law Review* 11:4 (2011): 758-773.
31. ECtHR, MSS v. Belgium and Greece, paras 252-254.
32. ECtHR, N.H. and others v. France (28820/13 75547/13 13114/15) 02/07/2020.
33. ECtHR, Hudorovič and others v. Slovenia (24816/14, 25140/14) 10/03/2020.
34. ECtHR, Price v. The UK (33394/96) 10/07/2001, ECtHR, V. v. The UK (24888/94) 12/16/1999, ECtHR, TM and CM v. The Republic of Moldova (26608/11) 01/28/2014 (para. 35).
35. ECtHR, Larioshina v. Russia (56869/00) 04/23/2002; Budina v. Russia (45603/05) 18/06/2009.
36. T. Françoise, *The European Convention on Human Rights and the Economic Crisis: The Issue of Poverty*. EUI Working Papers, AEL 2013/8; N. Napoletano, Estensione e limiti della dimensione

Indeed, these cases were later cited in the case on protection of migrants' social rights considered above.

Recently, Article 3 was referred to in the case concerning occupational health and safety. The case Mažukna v. Lithuania[37] was about the investigation into an accident at work. The applicant, a welder on a construction site, was disfigured having fallen from the scaffolding, which was broken. The pre-trial investigation into the accident took three years and seven months and the case was terminated as time-barred. The application was considered in light of procedural obligations of the state under Article 3, though the applicant initially made an application under Articles 6 and 13 of the Convention. The Court decided that the State violated Article 3 as there had not been an effective investigation into the circumstances of the accident in which the applicant was injured.[38] Article 3 imposes a procedural obligation to investigate and provide effective judicial and other remedies in response to an arguable claim of ill-treatment in breach of Article 3.[39] Therefore in order to fall within the ambit of procedural rules, the act itself should amount to inhuman or degrading treatment.[40] In our case, the negligent violation of Occupational Safety and Health (OSH) rules resulted in physical damages and the Court found that 'the situation attains the threshold of severity necessary to fall within the scope of Article 3 of the Convention'.[41] Thus the Court, stepping from its traditional strict views on the level of severity in the context of inhuman and degrading treatment, decided that the serious health impairment as a result of the accident at work is a form of degrading or/and inhuman treatment.

This approach of the Court is, in our opinion, very ambiguous[42] and should be supported by well-developed reasoning about the criteria which permitted the Court to conclude that the occupational accident had features of inhuman or degrading treatment. Traditionally, the Court refers to the concept of 'human dignity'[43] as the criterion of such treatment.[44] In this case, however, it is not evident that the dignity of the applicant was undermined.

This case evidences a remarkable extension of the scope of Article 3. First, it provides to all those who suffered in occupational accidents an additional ground for challenging the way of investigation and the provision of judicial remedy. Second, it can be interpreted as giving an opportunity to public employees to consider occupational accidents in light of positive obligations of the State under Article 3 of the ECHR. Such an opportunity was granted already under Article 2 if we will remember the case

economica e sociale della Convenzione europea dei diritti umani in tempi di crisi finanziaria, in *Diritti umani e diritto internazionale* 2:8 (2014).

37. ECtHR, Mažukna v. Lithuania (72092/12) 11/04/2017.
38. *Ibid.*, paras 85-87.
39. Harris, O'Boyle, Warbrick, *Law of the European Convention on Human Rights*. 2nd edn. Oxford University Press. Oxford 2009, 108.
40. Assenov and Others v. Bulgaria (90/1997/874/1086) 28/10/1998, E. and Others v. the United Kingdom (33218/96) 26/11/2002, MC v. Bulgaria (39272/98) 4/12/2003.
41. Mažukna v. Lithuania (No. 72092/12) 11/04/2017, para. 81.
42. *See also* the critics of the judgment in the dissenting opinion of Judge Bošnjak.
43. ECtHR, Bouyid v. Belgium [GC] (23380/09) 28/09/2015, para. 83.
44. *See also*, A. Reidy, *The Prohibition of Torture. A Guide to the Implementation of Article 3 of the European Convention on Human Rights*. Human rights Handbooks No. 6. Council of Europe (2003). Available at: https://rm.coe.int/168007ff4c.

Brincat v. Malta, which concerned the death of some employees of publicly owned shipyards as a result of the work with asbestos. In that case, the Court held that Article 2 laid down a positive obligation on States to take appropriate steps to safeguard the lives of those within their jurisdiction, including those who work in a public corporation owned and controlled by the Government. The present judgment in Mažukna v. Lithuania is a landmark decision expanding such an opportunity upon those who severely suffered in an occupational accident.

1.1.2 Interpretation of the Right to Respect for Private Life

According to Article 8 of the ECHR, everyone has the right to respect for his private and family life, his home and his correspondence. The absence of a definition of the concepts of private and family life left the Court free to interpret them broadly. The right to respect for private life now includes the right to protect one's reputation,[45] the right to establish and develop relationships with others,[46] and the right to be informed about the risks to which an employee is exposed in the workplace.[47]

Let us consider in more detail the right to develop relationships with other people. It was first formulated by the court in the judgment in Niemietz v. Germany,[48] which concerned the search of the lawyer's office. The Court noted that it did not consider it possible or necessary to give an exhaustive definition of the concept of 'private life' since it would be too strict to limit it to an intimate circle where everyone can live his own private life as he prefers, and thereby completely exclude the outside world from this circle. Respect for private life, according to the Court, must also include the right to establish and develop relationships with other people.

This conclusion of the Court later formed the basis of the decision in the Sidabras and Dziautas v. Lithuania case.[49] The applicants in the present case challenged the ban on employment in certain areas of the economy against former KGB officers. The Lithuanian government argued that the application should be declared inadmissible because the ECHR does not provide for a right to work. In response to this argument, the Court replied that the right to privacy should provide a person with a sphere within which he can freely develop and realize his abilities. Taking into account the experience of other countries in this area, the ECtHR found that the ban on the employment of former KGB officers violated the right to respect for the private life of these persons. It is interesting to note that in support of this conclusion, the ECtHR again cited the Airey v. Ireland decision on the absence of firm boundaries between the two blocks of rights,[50] and also referred to the norms of the ESC and the ILO Convention as a kind of rationale for the integration of the new right under the article.

45. ECtHR, Pfeifer v. Austria (12556/03) 11/15/2007, para. 35.
46. ECtHR, Niemietz v. Germany (13710/88) 12/16/1992, para. 29.
47. ECtHR, Vilnes and others v. Norway (52806/09 22703/10) 05/12/2013.
48. ECtHR, Niemietz v. Germany (13710/88)16/12/1992, para. 29.
49. ECtHR, Sidabras and Dziautas v. Lithuania.
50. ECtHR, Sidabras and Dziautas v. Lithuania (55480/00, 59330/00) 27/07/2004, para. 49.

In the case of Ukrainian Supreme Court judge, Oleksandr Volkov v. Ukraine,[51] the Court further developed the defence of the right to develop relationships with other people in cases of unfair dismissals. Violation of Article 8 of the ECHR, according to the ECtHR, in this case was due to the impact of the dismissal on the applicant's relations with a wide range of people, the material consequences of the dismissal that affected the well-being of his family, as well as damage to his professional reputation.

The protection of 'private social life'[52] is the new facet of Article 8, which appeared thanks to the integration of social rights into the ambit of the ECHR. It permitted the Court to consider not only the cases on unfair dismissals (*see* Chapter 4) but also the cases on employment discrimination under Article 14 in conjunction with Article 8 (*see* Chapter 3).

The integration of the right of citizens to develop relationships with other people can have great potential to overcome the shortcomings of the European system for the protection of socioeconomic rights, in particular in the field of dismissal protection. This approach, however, does not meet unanimity in the ECtHR. In one recent judgment,[53] already cited in the introduction, three judges signed the dissenting opinion, arguing that broad interpretation of Article 8 might lead to 'transforming a large number of labour law disputes into litigation for the protection of private life'. This case will be considered in more detail in the second part of the book. However, speaking about the integration of labour rights into the scope of the ECHR and responding to the precaution of the dissenting judges, it is necessary to refer to another citation of the Court. The ECtHR stated that when it comes to rights that have consequences of a social or economic nature, it is necessary, as well as with regard to the protection of civil and political rights, to strike a fair balance between the interests of society and the protection of fundamental rights of the individual.[54] We believe that this conclusion is extremely important for the applicants whose rights were not accurately balanced with the interests of society and where national legislation does not provide such a balancing exercise. As an illustration, we can refer to the case of the dismissal of a train driver for taking part in a strike by the applicant in 2018.[55] Russian law did not permit the strikes of train drivers, therefore, any work stoppage declared as a strike by these workers is illegal and no court (except for a Constitutional one) could evaluate the proportionality of the ban in question.

51. ECtHR, Oleksandr Volkov v. Ukraine (N 21722/11) 9.01.2013.
52. *See* Bigaeva v. Greece (26713/05) 28/05/2009; Bărbulescu v. Romania (61496/08) GC 05/09/2017.
53. ECtHR, Budimir v. Croatia (App No. 44691/14) 16/12/2021. This case concerned the withdrawal of the applicant's professional licence to work as a motor vehicle inspector, which the Court found to be an interference with his private life because without the licence, the applicant could not work and was dismissed.
54. ECtHR, AS v. Switzerland (39350/13) 06/30/2015, para. 31.
55. ECtHR, Ognevenko v. Russia, 20 November 2018, Application No. 44873/09.

1.2 THE VALUE OF ILO STANDARDS FOR ADJUDICATION OF LABOUR LAW CASES BY THE ECtHR[56]

It was mentioned before that the reference to other international treaties is the method permitting to integrate new rights relating to labour into the scope of ECHR. The rights provided in the Convention are left without definition, therefore, many of them should be understood in line with other international human rights instruments to ensure a more universal and harmonious protection. The general basis for the ability to refer to other international instruments in its deliberations was acknowledged in Cudak v. Lithuania: 'The Convention, including Article 6, cannot be interpreted in a vacuum. The Court must therefore be mindful of the Convention's special character as a human rights treaty, and it must also take the relevant rules of international law into account.'[57] The Vienna Convention on the Law of Treaties fixed the possibility to refer to 'other relevant rules of international law' for the interpretation of international treaties (Article 31.3 (C)). The direct reference to this discretion can be found in numerous labour law cases.[58] In the famous Demir and Baikara v. Turkey case, the ECtHR stated the following: 'The Court, in defining the meaning of terms and notions in the text of the Convention, *can and must* take into account elements of international law other than the Convention, the interpretation of such elements by competent organs, and the practice of European States reflecting their common values. In this context, it is not necessary for the respondent State to have ratified the entire collection of instruments that are applicable in respect of the precise subject matter of the case concerned. It will be sufficient for the Court that the relevant international instruments denote a continuous evolution in the norms and principles applied in international law or in the domestic law of the majority of member States of the Council of Europe and show, in a precise area, that there is common ground in modern societies.'[59]

Thus, the Court went even beyond the norms of the Vienna Convention, permitting itself to take into account also those pieces of international law which were not ratified by the responding state. In this context, the reference to the ILO Conventions and instruments is particularly valuable for the Court. ILO is a key expert organization in the field of labour rights; it includes almost the same quantity of states as the UN and thus ensures almost universal coverage of its Constitution and the fundamental labour standards. It is also very important that international labour standards are adopted by the International Labour Conference, uniting workers, employers and governments. The Committee on Freedom of Association (CFA), the ILO monitoring body whose conclusions are often cited by the Court in the cases on the freedom of association, is also organized on a tripartite basis. Tripartism ensures a

56. This part is largely based on the work previously published in E. Sychenko, 'ILO Contributions to the Jurisprudence of International Human Rights Bodies'. *Zbornik Pravnog fakulteta u Zagrebu* 71:6 (2021): 897-920.
57. ECtHR, Cudak v. Lithuania (No. 15869/02), 23 March 2010, para. 56.
58. ECtHR, R.M.T. v. The UK (31045/10) 8 April 2014, para. 76; Demir and Baikara v. Turkey, para. 65, Cudak v. Lithuania, para. 56.
59. ECtHR, Demir and Baikara v. Turkey, paras 85-86.

greater legitimacy of the standards and their support by social partners.[60] This point is also important for establishing the content of human rights at work by the ECtHR.

Scholars affirmed that ILO standards serve as a source of legitimacy and interpretative guidance for regional human rights courts[61] and that they help to contextualize human rights questions in the employment sphere.[62]

The references to the international labour standards permit the Court to develop the interpretation of the Convention to ensure the protection of certain labour rights. The examples of the integration of new rights are numerous: the right for collective bargaining,[63] the right for a strike,[64] the right to access information concerning risks the employee is exposed to,[65] the right to be reinstated in case of unfair dismissal,[66] and the right for the strike of solidarity.[67]

Magdalena Forowicz, the author of profound research on the consideration of international law by the ECtHR, noted that the ECtHR finds itself at the apex of two diametrically different judicial paradigms: an open paradigm characterized by a high level of judicial activism and unhindered references to international law; and a closed paradigm marked by judicial restraint and few references to international law.[68] The so-called open paradigm might very often be found in labour-related cases, particularly those related to Articles 4 (forced labour) and 11 (freedom of association). In these cases, the ECtHR always refers to the ILO Conventions and, more rarely, to the conclusions of the ILO bodies. It was noted that the ECtHR benefits from the specialization, a century-long experience of the ILO and the distinctive legitimacy of its standards and supervisory bodies, particularly, in the field of anti-discrimination case law.[69] Scholars assume that the references to the ILO standards enable the ECtHR to fill certain gaps in the text of the ECHR.[70] Indeed, key notions of those articles are not defined in the text of the ECHR – forced labour and the freedom of association.

60. *See*, e.g., K. Curtis, '100 Years of the ILO in Action: Reflections on Inclusive Collective Representation and the Organization's Quest for Social Justice'. *King's Law Journal* 32:2 (2021): 184.
61. F. Ebert & V. Oelz, 'Bridging the Gap Between Labour Rights and Human Rights: The Role of ILO Law in Regional Human Rights Courts'. *ILO* International Institute for Labour Studies, Geneva. 2012.
62. V. Mantouvalou, 'Labour Rights in the European Convention on Human Rights: An Intellectual Justification for an Integrated Approach to Interpretation'. *Human Rights Law Review* 13:3 (2013): 529-555.
63. ECtHR, Demir and Baykara v. Turkey (34503/97) Grand chamber, 12 November 2008.
64. ECtHR, ENERJI Yapi-Yol Sen c. Turquie (68959/01), 21/04/2009.
65. ECtHR, Brincat and others v. Malta (60908/11, 62110/11, 62129/11, 62312/11, 62338/11) 24 July 2014.
66. ECtHR, Oleksandr Volkov v. Ukraine (21722/11) 9.01.2013.
67. ECtHR, the National union of rail, maritime and transport workers v. The United Kingdom (31045/10) 08/04/2014, para. 86.
68. *Ibid.*, p. 4.
69. Tzehainesh Teklè, 'The Contribution of the ILO's International Labour Standards System to the European Court of Human Rights' Jurisprudence in the Field of Non-discrimination'. *Industrial Law Journal* 49:1 (2020): 86-112, https://doi.org/10.1093/indlaw/dwz020.
70. *See* more on earlier references of the ECtHR to the ILO and ESC standards in J. Merrills, *The Development of International Law by the European Court of Human Rights*. Manchester University Press. Manchester 1988, 202-203.

Therefore, the ECtHR defines these notions and the content of the freedom of association through references to the ILO standards.

For example, forced labour, prohibited under Article 4 of the ECHR, is defined by the ECtHR in light of the ILO Convention No. 29 concerning forced or compulsory labour.[71] ILO Convention No. 29 on Forced or Compulsory Labour has been cited in all the cases considered to date under Article 4-2 of the ECHR. According to this instrument, the term forced or compulsory labour means all work or service which is exacted from any person under the menace of any penalty and for which the said person has not offered himself voluntarily. ILO Convention No. 29 lists the types of work that are excluded from the term 'forced and compulsory labour'. This list provided in Article 4-3 of the ECHR is largely analogous. However, in contrast with the ILO instrument, the ECHR lacks the precision of the meaning of 'emergency' used in this article.

In the case of Chitos v. Greece,[72] the ECtHR used the reference to the ILO Convention No. 29 to justify its reading of the provision of Article 4-3(b) as covering only compulsory military service. This article lists those types of activities that cannot be considered forced labour. The applicant, an army officer, argued that the obligation to pay a fee to the State to resign before the end of his period of service constituted forced labour. Therefore, this case was a significant opportunity for the ECtHR to delimit specifically the exceptions covered by Article 4-3(b). The ECtHR referred to the ESC, the ILO Convention No. 29 and Recommendation CM/Rec (2010) 4 of the Committee of Ministers to the Member States on Human Rights of Members of the Armed Forces.

The lack of definition of the right to the freedom of association makes the ECtHR refer to the relevant provisions of the ILO Conventions, the ESC and the opinions of ILO bodies and the European Committee of Social Rights.[73] The analysis of these sources, for instance, made the ECtHR conclude the existence of 'core'[74] and 'additional' collective rights.[75] These international sources aid the ECtHR in its interpretation work, also concerning the possible restriction of the freedom of association, set out in Part 2 of Article 11. For example, in the case Tymoshenko and others v. Ukraine,[76] the ECtHR had to ascertain whether the 'interests of national security or public safety or the protection of health or morals or the rights and freedoms of others' might justify the prohibition of strikes by pilots of a private company. The ECtHR used references to the

71. ECtHR, Van Der Mussele v. Belgium (8919/80) 23/11/1983, Siliadin v. France (73316/01) 26/07/2005, Stummer v. Austria (37452/02) 07/07/2011, Graziani-Weiss v. Austria (31950/06) 18.10.2011.
72. ECtHR, Chitos v. Greece (51637/12) 4 June 2015.
73. ECtHR, Trade Union of the Police in the Slovak Republic and Others v. Slovakia (11828/08) 25/09/2012, para. 53, Vörđur Ólafsson v. Iceland (20161/06) 27/04/2010, para. 38, Associated Society of Locomotive Engineers and Firemen (ASLEF) v. The United Kingdom (11002/05) 27/02/2007, para. 67, ECtHR, Veniamin Tymoshenko and others v. Ukraine (48408/12) 02/10/2014.
74. The right for collective bargaining, the negative freedom of association, *see* Demir and Baikara, Sorensen and Rasmussen v. Denmark [GC] (52562/99 52620/99) 11/01/2006.
75. For example, the right for the solidarity strike, *see* ECtHR, R.M.T. v. the UK (31045/10) 08/04/2014.
76. ECtHR, Veniamin Tymoshenko and Others v. Ukraine (48408/12) 02/10/2014.

provisions of ILO Conventions and the ESC to show that the derogative clause must be read in a restrictive way.[77]

Considering the question about the right to collective bargaining of the municipal servants under Article 11 of the ECHR, the Court referred to the provisions of the ILO Conventions Nos 87 and 98, No. 151. It also referred to the opinion of the Committee of Experts on the Application of Conventions and Recommendations (CEACR) to underline that only those officials who are directly employed in the administration of the State are excluded from the scope of Convention No. 98 (paragraphs 43-44). CEACR pointed out that the only admissible exception to the right to organize might be in respect of the armed forces and the police. The reference to the CEACR's concluding observation was used by the ECtHR to demonstrate that ILO has already evaluated the situation in Turkey and, taking into account that it was cited in the final part of the judgment, that the Court rather agrees with this position (paragraphs 101-102).

The right to strike is another sphere where the ECtHR always refers to the ILO. This right is not mentioned in the text of Article 11 and was deduced by the Court from 'the right to form and to join trade unions for the protection of his interests'. Interestingly, in the first cases concerning the right to strike, the Court refrained from citing or referring to the ILO's legal positions. No mention might be found in Schmidt and Dahlström v. Sweden, where it was stated that Article 11 leaves each State a free choice of the means to be used for the protection of trade unions' rights, 'the grant of a right to strike represents without any doubt one of the most important of these means, but there are others'.[78] Despite the fact that the right to strike by 1976 was already recognized by the ILO bodies, for example, in the Resolution of the International Labour Conference concerning the Abolition of Anti-Trade Union Legislation in the States Members of the International Labour Organisation, adopted in 1957. It called for the adoption of 'laws ... ensuring the effective and unrestricted exercise of trade union rights, including the right to strike, by the workers'.[79] In 1976, the ECtHR found the application concerning the right to strike inadmissible.

Ed Bated, the author of a very interesting research on the history of the ECtHR, argues that the Court 'matured' with the years and became much bolder in its interpretation since the 1990s.[80] This trend might be traced in the case law on strikes. Almost thirty years after the Schmidt and Dahlström decision, where no reference to the ILO might be found, the Court again had to consider the restrictions of the right to strike. In Enerji Yapi-Yol Sen v. Turkey, it stated that the strike was an important aspect for union members in protecting their interests, that it was recognized by the supervisory bodies of the ILO as 'the inseparable corollary of the right to organize' and is protected by the ILO Convention C87 on freedom of association and protection of the

77. *Ibid.*, paras 32-49.
78. ECtHR, Schmidt and Dahlström v. Sweden (5589/72) 06/02/1976.
79. B. Gernigon, A. Odero and H. Guido, 'ILO Principles Concerning the Right to Strike'. *International Labour Review* 137:4 (1998), https://www.ilo.org/wcmsp5/groups/public/---ed_norm/---normes/documents/publication/wcms_087987.pdf.
80. E. Bates, *The Evolution of the European Convention on Human Rights: From Its Inception to the Creation of a Permanent Court of Human Rights*. Oxford University Press. New York 2010, 435.

right to organize.[81] In 2009, it found that banning a one-day public sector workers' strike violated Article 11.

After five years, in 2014, the Court considered the famous case National Union of Rail, Maritime and Transport Workers v. the United Kingdom,[82] where the arguments of the applicant union substantiating the argument that the ban of the secondary strikes violated the freedom of association provided in Article 11 of the ECHR, was substantiated mostly by the references to ILO Conventions, and the interpretation given to them by the ILO bodies (paragraphs 27-33). The Court throughout the judgment considered the positions of the ILO on this point, establishing that that secondary action was recognized and protected as part of trade-union freedom under ILO Convention No. 87. Further, it stressed though that its jurisdiction was limited to the ECHR and that it had no competence to assess the respondent State's compliance with the relevant standards of the ILO containing a 'more specific and exacting norm regarding industrial action'.[83] The latter stance of the Court seems to be a caution against too much reliance on the ILO standards. The Court might refer to ILO positions but they do not form obligatory lines of reasoning, rather a kind of the practical framework for the reflection.

In a more recent case on a right to strike - Ognevenko v. Russia - the *Court* extensively cited the ILO's positions on the limits to the right to strike. The case was about the dismissal of a train driver for taking part in a strike. The strike for railway staff is prohibited by the Federal Law of 10 January 2003 No. 17-FZ 'On Railway Transport in Russia'. The Court considered the opinions of the CFA and the CEACR,[84] who were unanimous in the definition of essential services and in urging Russia to amend the legislation prohibiting strikes for railway staff.[85]

Relying on a very developed jurisprudence of the CFA is a win-win method, ensuring support of the judgment from the part of the experts and harmonious reading of the norm in line with other international instruments. Such a reading is particularly needed in relation to the right to strike when this right[86] is contested by the employer's representatives at the ILO.[87]

It should be particularly emphasized that the reference of the ECtHR to the positions of the ILO bodies on the right to strike and the explicit recognition of this right as a part of the freedom of association is very important in the situation when the

81. ECtHR, Enerji Yapi-Yol Sen v. Turkey (68959/01) 21/04/2009.
82. ECtHR, The R.M.T. v. United Kingdom (31045/10) 08/04/2014.
83. ECtHR, The National Union of Rail, Maritime and Transport Workers v. the UK (31045/10)08/04/2014, para. 106.
84. ECtHR, Ognevenko v. Russia 20 November 2018, Application No. 44873/09, paras 20-23, 26.
85. *See* note 2 above.
86. ECtHR, Enerji Yapi-Yol Sen c. Turquie (N 68959/01), 21/04/2009.
87. E. Gerasimova and S. Kolganova, 'The Right for Strike in ILO Jurisprudence: Crisis of Recognition?'. *Law Journal of the Higher School of Economics* 4 (2016): 184-197; L. Swepston, 'Crisis in the ILO Supervisory System: Dispute over the Right to Strike'. *International Journal of Comparative Labour Law and Industrial Relations* 2 (2013): 199-218.

employers' representatives at the ILO deny the fact that strikes are regulated by ILO Conventions.[88]

The Ognevenko case is another contribution of the ECtHR to the support of the right to strike on the international level. It is the first binding judgment of the human rights body, which indirectly acknowledges that the general prohibition of strikes for the railway staff is incompatible with the human rights standards, namely with Article 11 of the ECHR. It is an example of the interconnection between the human rights instrument - ECHR - and the ILO standards. It demonstrates that the human rights bodies seek to develop not only a common understanding of human rights among UN agencies[89] but also a kind of global common understanding between UN and regional human rights bodies.

Concluding this chapter, there is a need to underline the following points: the will of the Court to treat human rights as indivisible and the integration of labour rights and human rights at work to the scope of the ECHR might be seen as an attempt to overcome the weakness of the system of social rights protection in the Council of Europe. The ILO standards are used by the Court to fill the gaps in the Convention through the use of ILO concepts and standards for the regulation of the different aspects of the working conditions. The reference to the positions of the ILO bodies (CFA, CEACR) is also a method legitimizing the living interpretation of the ECHR.

88. R. Hornung-Draus, 'The Right to Strike in the ILO System of Standards: Facts and Fiction'. *Comparative Labour Law and Policy Journal* 39:3 (2018): 531-536.
89. *See* UN Statement of Common Understanding on Human Rights-Based Approaches to Development Cooperation and Programming, 2003.

CHAPTER 2

The Prohibition of Slavery, Servitude, Forced or Compulsory Labour

ARTICLE 4. Prohibition of slavery and forced labour

1. No one shall be held in slavery or servitude.
2. No one shall be required to perform forced or compulsory labour.
3. For the purpose of this Article the term 'forced or compulsory labour' shall not include: (a) any work required to be done in the ordinary course of detention imposed according to the provisions of Article 5 of this Convention or during conditional release from such detention; (b) any service of a military character or, in case of conscientious objectors in countries where they are recognised, service exacted instead of compulsory military service; (c) any service exacted in case of an emergency or calamity threatening the life or well-being of the community; (d) any work or service which forms part of normal civic obligations.

The text of Article 4 of the ECHR prohibits slavery, servitude, forced and compulsory labour without defining these offences. The definitions are taken from the ILO Convention No. 29, as it was demonstrated in the previous chapter. According to the approach of the ECHR, this article creates both positive and negative obligations that States must comply with. The negative one – not to enslave and not to engage people in other forms of forced labour – is really referred to in the jurisprudence of the Court. The majority of cases are based on alleged non-compliance with the positive obligations. For example, the States were held liable as they failed to establish an effective system granting protection and remedy to the applicants in the circumstances of domestic servitude.[90] The ECtHR has stated that the States must enact domestic law criminalizing slavery, involuntary servitude and forced labour to ensure the effective prosecution of such crimes.[91] It also required a certain quality of investigation of such

90. ECtHR, C.N. and V. v. France (67724/09) 11 October 2012; ECtHR, C.N. v. The United Kingdom (4239/08) 13 November 2012.
91. ECtHR, Siliadin v. France (73316/01) 26 July 2005, paras 89, 112.

crimes.[92] In the period 2017-2021, the Court considered a number of cases under Article 4, further developing its requirements for the positive obligations of States. Below, we will consider those cases in a retrospective way.

J. and others v. Austria,[93] considered in 2017, concerned the state's duty to investigate the cases of forced or compulsory labour. In this case, two Filipino nationals, who had gone to work as maids or au pairs in the United Arab Emirates, alleged that their employers had taken their passports away from them and exploited them also during their stay in Austria until the moment when the applicants managed to escape. In their opinion, the decision of Austrian authorities to discontinue the investigation into the applicants' case concerning the events in Austria was in violation of Article 4 of the Convention. The Court noted that the States were not required under Article 4 to provide for universal jurisdiction over trafficking offences committed abroad and that Austrian authorities had taken all necessary steps which could have reasonably been expected in the situation, in particular taking into account that the applicants applied to the police approximately one year after the escape when their employers had long left the country.

The scholars emphasized that 'the case did provide the Court with an opportunity to frame in very lucid and firm terms that Article 4 of the ECHR generates a positive obligation upon states to identify and support (potential) victims of trafficking and for this purpose states have to build a legal and administrative framework'.[94] Indeed, the Court referred to the following acts of the Government, which, in its opinion, constituted compliance with this positive obligation: applicants were immediately treated as (potential) victims of human trafficking; they were interviewed by specially trained police officers; they were granted residence and work permits in order to regularize their stay in Austria; a personal data disclosure ban was imposed on the Central Register so their whereabouts were untraceable by the general public; during the domestic proceedings, the applicants were supported by the NGO LEFÖ, which is funded by the Government especially to provide assistance to victims of human trafficking; the applicants were given legal representation, procedural guidance and assistance to facilitate their integration in Austria. All these measures are foreseen in the Council of Europe Convention on Action against Trafficking in Human Beings and in Protocol No. 29 to the ILO Forced Labour Convention. The latter, together with the ILO Recommendation No. 203 was also mentioned in the footnote of the decision, which, however, has not been referred to in the text.[95]

This judgment was welcomed by scholars as a strengthening of states' obligation to identify victims of human trafficking.[96]

92. ECtHR, Rantsev v. Cyprus and Russia (25965/04) 7 January 2010, para. 288.
93. ECtHR, J. and others v. Austria (58216/12) 17.01.2017.
94. Stoyanova Vladislava, J. and others v. Austria and *the* strengthening *of states' obligation to identify victims of human trafficking*, 7 February 2017, https://strasbourgobservers.com/2017/02/07/j-and-others-v-austria-and-the-strengthening-of-states-obligation-to-identify-victims-of-human-trafficking/.
95. J. and others v. Austria, note 3.
96. *Ibid.*

Also in 2017, the ECHR considered the application of 'workers' who could leave their place of work and move freely in the area, but these factors did not prevent the court from recognizing a violation of Article 4 of the ECHR. The application in Chowdury and Others v. Greece[97] was made by forty-two Bangladeshi citizens who were gathering strawberries on the farm under the supervision of armed guards. They voluntarily entered into an employment relationship, were provided with food and accommodation and were able to move freely around the territory. The employer did not pay them for six months and warned them that they would only receive their earnings if they continued to work.

This case is extremely interesting because the Court has broadened the interpretation of forced labour and human trafficking. In fact, the ECHR does not provide a definition of human trafficking. However, the Court, in its earlier decisions, concluded that trafficking in human beings falls under the prohibition of Article 4 of the ECHR as it is one of the forms of forced labour and constitutes modern slavery.[98]

The difficulty in qualifying the actions of the 'employer' in this case was due to the fact that the plaintiffs voluntarily agreed to do the work and were free to leave the place. The Court held that the original consent to employment 'is not sufficient to exclude the qualification of the relationship as forced labour'.[99] It was noted that voluntary consent is only one factor to be taken into consideration in light of all the circumstances of the case. The ECtHR further drew attention to the vulnerable situation of Bangladeshi workers, as they were illegal migrants and could not avail themselves of legal remedies to protect their rights, as well as to the appalling working and living conditions described in the Greek court's decision. They had lived in makeshift huts made of cardboard, nylon and bamboo without a toilet or water supply; their employers had not paid them and had warned them that they would only receive their wages if they continued to work.[100]

In this case, the Court analysed the provisions of the Convention on Action against Trafficking in Human Beings adopted by the Council of Europe.[101] The ECtHR held that if an employer abused its rights or exploited the vulnerability of its employees, it meant that they did not accept voluntary employment.[102]

This judgment demonstrates that the concept of forced labour is now interpreted by the Court to also include non-payment of wage arrears when 'workers' are in a vulnerable position. The vulnerability of the applicants was established on the basis of several factors: they were deprived of any recourse; they could have been deported as illegal immigrants; and they were deprived of any means and housing. In our opinion,

97. ECtHR, Chowdury and Others v. Greece (21884/15) 30.03.2017.
98. ECtHR, Rantsev v. Cyprus and Russia (25965/04) 07/01/2010, R. Pati, 'States' Positive Obligations with Respect to Human Trafficking: ECtHR Breaks New Ground in Rantsev v. Cyprus & Russia'. *Boston University International Law Journal* 29:1 (2011): 141.
99. Chowdury and Others v. Greece, para. 96.
100. *Ibid.*, para. 93.
101. https://www.coe.int/ru/web/conventions/full-list/-/conventions/treaty/197 (accessed 20 May 2020).
102. Chowdury and Others v. Greece, para. 96.

the combination of these factors in their entirety has led the Court to conclude that the employer's actions were forced or compulsory labour.

Having established that the actions against the claimants amounted to human trafficking, banned under Article 4 of the ECHR, the Court continued to assess whether the national authorities had fulfilled their positive obligations in providing due protection for the victims and the effective investigation of the case. Greece was found to have substantially fulfilled its obligation to establish a legal framework to combat trafficking in persons, but the measures taken by the authorities to prevent trafficking were insufficient. The Court considered that the local police station was aware of the employers' refusal to pay the applicants' salaries, but had not taken timely measures to protect them and that the national court had interpreted the concept of trafficking in human beings in a narrow manner, thus acquitting the defendants. The Greek Court found that the fact that the complainants had freedom of movement showed no signs of forced labour. It should be noted that this approach is characteristic of some other states. For example, in Russia, the courts never consider that human trafficking takes place when the victim had any freedom of movement.[103]

Broadening of the understanding of forced labour in this case through 'allowing the most serious cases of exploitation'[104] to be considered under Article 4, the legal position of the Court that neither the original consent to employment nor the freedom to leave the place of exploitation[105] are not sufficient to exclude the qualification of the relationship as forced labour are the key points of this judgment. This legal reasoning might be particularly valuable for the national lawyers and law-enforcement bodies of the Council of Europe. Also, this case made clear that we need to consider the situation of exploitation as a whole and assess every case individually.[106] Finally, this case contributes to understanding the borderline between bad labour conditions and exploitation. Based on these judgments, the scholars proposed three key factors that play a role in defining the tipping point between the two: control (including coercion) over the worker, vulnerability, and consent.[107]

The case S.M. v. Croatia,[108] considered by the Chamber in 2018 and by the Grand Chamber in 2020, is another interesting example of further broadening of the Court's perception of acts prohibited under Article 4 and clear inclusion of human trafficking to its ambit.

103. *See* E. Sychenko, V. Gracheva & M. Rodichev. 'Modern Slavery in Russia: Exploitation Without Chains'. *Italian Labour Law e-Journal* 14:1 (2021): 261-274.
104. A. Lucifora, 'From Old Slavery to New Forms of Exploitation: A Reflection on the Conditions of Irregular Migrant Labour After the Chowdury Case'. *New Journal of European Criminal Law* 10:3 (2019): 251-267.
105. The Court stated that restrictions upon freedom of movement cannot be a necessary element for qualifying a situation as forced labour (Chowdury and Others v. Greece, para. 123).
106. D. Mccann and J. Fudge, 'Unacceptable Forms of Work: A Multidimensional Model'. *International Labour Review* 156:2 (2017): 147-184.
107. C. Rijken, 'When Bad Labour Conditions Become Exploitation', in: Conny Rijken and Tesseltje de Lange (eds) *Towards a Decent Labour Market for Low-Waged Migrant Workers*. Amsterdam University Press B.V., Amsterdam, 2018, 189-206. Available at, https://library.oapen.org/bitstream/handle/20.500.12657/28269/1/1001707.pdf#page=190.
108. ECtHR, S.M. v. Croatia (application No. 60561/14) 19/07/2018.

The case concerned a Croatian woman's complaint that she had been forced into prostitution. She lodged a criminal complaint in September 2012, alleging that a man had forced her into prostitution over several months in mid-2011, had made her give him half of the money she had earned from providing sexual services and had threatened her and punished her if she did not comply with his demands. At the end of 2012, the man was indicted and the applicant was officially given the status of victim of human trafficking. He was further acquitted of forcing the applicant into prostitution as the prosecution had failed to provide sufficient evidence for a conviction, and the courts found that the applicant had given sexual services voluntarily.

The applicant complained of the inadequacy of the domestic legal framework and the lack of adequate procedural response from the domestic authorities to her allegations that she had been pressured into or exploited through prostitution, she relied on Articles 3, 4 and 8 of the Convention. The Court, though, decided to examine her complaints under Article 4 of the Convention only.

Article 4 says nothing about human trafficking, but the Court has expanded it upon this crime in Rantsev v. Cyprus and Russia[109] and in the mentioned case Chowdury v. Greece.[110] In this case, the applicant was granted the status of the victim of human trafficking and necessary protection. National courts, having considered the criminal case on forced prostitution established that she has provided the sexual services voluntarily.

Hence in our opinion, the ECtHR had to provide a solid explanation for the consideration of this case under Article 4. The Chamber judgment includes a number of rather vague lines which were supposed to provide this justification. In particular, the Court pointed out:

> There can be no doubt that trafficking and exploitation of prostitution threaten the human dignity and fundamental freedoms of its victims and cannot be considered compatible with a democratic society and the values expounded in the Convention. In view of its obligation to interpret the Convention in the light of present-day conditions, the Court considers it unnecessary to identify whether the treatment of which the applicant complained constituted 'slavery', 'servitude' or 'forced and compulsory labour'. Instead, the Court concludes that trafficking itself as well as exploitation of prostitution ... fall within the scope of Article 4 of the Convention and will assess the present case under that provision.

This stance makes us question if since this case any other acts that 'threaten the human dignity and fundamental freedoms' might be considered under Article 4 without any reflection if they constitute one of the prohibited acts as 'slavery', 'servitude' or 'forced and compulsory labour'. Can the obligation to interpret the Convention in the light of present-day conditions be understood as an incentive for Court's too-active judicial activism?

We suppose that, taking into account the facts of the case, the Court might have provided a different justification for the consideration of the case under Article 4. The applicant claimed the presence of all three factors of human trafficking: action, means,

109. ECtHR, Rantsev v. Cyprus and Russia.
110. ECtHR, Chowdury and Others v. Greece (21884/15)30.03.2017.

and purpose.[111] However, the means factor (coercion) was not proved during the national proceedings.[112] The reasoning of the ECtHR in the present case may be summed up in the following way: as the applicant asserted to be the victim of human trafficking, the State had to investigate thoroughly the facts, interrogating those people who might help to establish the means factor: the clients, the neighbours and those people who helped her to escape. National courts came to the conclusion that she had provided the sexual services voluntarily without interviewing those people, therefore the State did not fulfil their procedural obligations under Article 4 of the Convention. Thus we assume that this case was correctly considered in light of Article 4 as the State did not effectively investigate the alleged case of human trafficking.

The ECHR pointed out that according to Croatian law, the United Nations Convention for the Suppression of the Traffic in Persons and the Exploitation of the Prostitution of Others and the Council of Europe Anti-trafficking Convention, the consent of the victim is irrelevant in cases of human trafficking. Dissenting Judge Koskelo expressed an opinion that this finding in the context of the case is a misconception of the norm. The norm in question entails that 'where coercion or another form of the "means" element of trafficking has been established, the victim's consent is incapable of operating as a valid defence to the effect of exonerating the perpetrator'.[113] Indeed coercion is a crucial element to determine human trafficking. Article 4 of the Council of Europe Convention on Action against Trafficking in Human Beings defines this phenomenon as the recruitment, transportation, transfer, harbouring or receipt of persons, *by means of the threat or use of force or other forms of coercion, of abduction, of fraud, of deception, of the abuse of power or of a position of vulnerability* ... for the purpose of exploitation. All the acts enumerated in italics represent different forms of coercion. Further Article 4 states that the consent of a victim of 'trafficking in human beings' to the intended exploitation shall be irrelevant *where any of the means set forth above have been used.* Accordingly, the *further* consent of the victim is irrelevant. But, as provided in the case, the State did not interrogate the first client of the applicant, or any other clients, as well as people living close to the applicant who might have confirmed her words.

The case was reconsidered by the Grand Chamber two years later. Scholars note that 'the referral of the case to the Grand Chamber has to be viewed in light of the powerful and convincing dissenting opinion of Judge Koskelo', given the 'definitional quagmire that the various Chamber judgments under Article 4 have caused'.[114] In the Grand Chamber judgment, the Court provided reasoning for the inclusion of human trafficking under Article 4 ECHR (paragraphs 286-297) and further substantiated the inclusion of forced prostitution under Article 4 (paragraphs 298-302).

111. J. Elliott, *The Role of Consent in Human Trafficking*. Routledge, New York, 2014.
112. ECtHR, S.M. v. Croatia, para. 18.
113. Dissenting Opinion of Judge Koskelo, para. 38.
114. S. Vladislava, *The Grand Chamber Judgment in S.M. v Croatia: Human Trafficking, Prostitution and the Definitional Scope of Article 4 ECHR*. 3 July 2020. Available at, https://strasbourgobservers.com/2020/07/03/the-grand-chamber-judgment-in-s-m-v-croatia-human-trafficking-prostitution-and-the-definitional-scope-of-article-4-echr/ (accessed 20 June 2021).

In the part dedicated to human trafficking, the Court cited the legal reasoning exposed in the Rantsev case (*see* paragraphs cited above) and concluded that as 'the Convention itself does not define the concept of human trafficking, it is not possible to characterize conduct or a situation as an issue of human trafficking unless it fulfils the criteria established for that phenomenon in international law'. Referring to international law, the Court pointed to the Palermo Protocol[115] and the Council of Europe Convention on Action against Trafficking in Human Beings. The former instrument, however, covers only transnational human trafficking involving an organized criminal group.

Surprisingly, in this part, the Court did not refer to Protocol No. 29 (P29) to the ILO Forced Labour Convention, 1930. It was adopted in 2014 and came into force in 2016. The Preamble of the P29 states that 'the context and forms of forced or compulsory labour have changed and trafficking in persons for forced or compulsory labour, which may involve sexual exploitation, is the subject of growing international concern and requires urgent action for its effective elimination'. Article 1 of the P29 called for the inclusion of specific action against trafficking of persons for forced or compulsory labour. The Palermo Protocol was mentioned as a relevant international instrument in the Preamble to P29. Thus, we suppose that the definition of human trafficking set in the Palermo Protocol should also be used in those countries which adopted P29. At present, less than half of the members of the Council of Europe ratified this ILO Protocol,[116] while the Council of Europe Convention on Action against Trafficking in Human Beings was ratified by all but three members.[117]

We suppose that a stronger emphasis on the development of the ILO approach to the issue of forced labour as expressed in the P29 might provide an additional argument for the consideration of human trafficking under Article 4. Here we have to recall that the definition of forced labour by the ECtHR was always made through the reference to the ILO Forced Labour Convention. The reference to this convention may be also found in the annex to the Preparatory work on Article 4.[118] The adoption of the Protocol to this Convention, which requires the states to suppress forced labour in all of its forms including human trafficking, to take effective measures to prevent and eliminate its use, to provide to victims protection and access to appropriate and effective remedies, such as compensation, and to sanction the perpetrators of forced labour, celebrates the evolution of the international approach to the obligations of the states in this field. It

115. Protocol to Prevent, Suppress and Punish Trafficking in Persons, Especially Women and Children, supplementing the United Nations Convention against Transnational Organized Crime, adopted 15 November 2000.
116. *See* a list of ratifications, https://www.ilo.org/dyn/normlex/en/f?p = NORMLEXPUB:11300:0::NO:11300:P11300_INSTRUMENT_ID:3174672:NO (accessed 20 June 2021).
117. It is open for ratification also for non-members of the CoE, Belarus and Israel ratified this Convention. *See* the list of ratifications, https://www.coe.int/en/web/conventions/full-list/-/conventions/treaty/197/signatures?module = signatures-by-treaty&treatynum = 197 (accessed 20 June 2021).
118. *See* Preparatory work on Article 4 of the Convention. Council of Europe. 1962. 3, available at, http://www.echr.coe.int/LibraryDocs/Travaux/ECHRTravaux-ART4-DH(62)10-BIL1712017.PDF (accessed 1 January 2015).

might have been referred to in S.M. v. Croatia as an illustration of the development of international law.[119]

The inclusion of the exploitation of prostitution within the scope of Article 4 of the ECHR was another controversial point of the Chamber judgment which was criticized in the dissenting opinion of Judge Koskelo. In the Grand Chamber judgment, the Court stated that only forced prostitution might fall within the scope of Article 4. It stressed that 'force' may encompass the subtle forms of coercive conduct identified in the Court's case law on Article 4, as well as by the ILO and in other international materials (paragraph 301).

Finally, the Court outlined the list of positive obligations under Article 4: (i) the duty to put in place a legislative and administrative framework to prohibit and punish trafficking; (ii) the duty, in certain circumstances, to take operational measures to protect victims, or potential victims, of trafficking; and (iii) a procedural obligation to investigate situations of potential trafficking (paragraph 306). These obligations reflect the approaches of Palermo protocol as well as ILO Protocol N 29 and CoE Anti-Trafficking Convention to the prevention of human trafficking and protection of victims.

The Court established multiple shortcomings in the conduct of the case, such as the non-questioning of certain witnesses, and the lack of investigation of the circumstances of the first contact between the applicant and the alleged perpetrator. These shortcomings, in the opinion of the Court, 'fundamentally undermined the domestic authorities' ability to determine whether the applicant had been exploited as she alleged'. It concluded that there were significant flaws in the domestic authorities' procedural response to the arguable claim and prima facie evidence that the applicant had been subjected to treatment contrary to Article 4 of the Convention (paragraph 346).

Summing up the consideration of this Grand Chamber judgment, there is a need to emphasize the obligation of the states to investigate properly the presence of coercion and interrogate all those people who, according to the victims' submissions, might witness the existence of the 'means factor' of human trafficking. It again urges the States Parties of the Council of Europe to efficiently implement the norms prohibiting human trafficking and ensure the effective investigation of this crime.[120] This judgment is an important contribution to the struggle with forced prostitution. Bringing these cases into the scope of Article 4 of the ECHR, the Court urges the States to investigate properly the presence of coercion and interrogate all those people who, according to the victim's submission, might witness the existence of the 'means factor' of human trafficking. It also offers clarity on the definition of 'human trafficking' and

119. This Protocol was mentioned by the Court in the part dedicated to the review of relevant international law (paras 148-151); the brief reference to this Protocol might also be found in the footnote to the decision in J. and others v. Austria (58216/12) 17/01/2017, the decision of inadmissibility (para. 2).

120. *See also* G. Kane, 'Building a House upon Sand? Human Trafficking, Forced Labor, and Exploitation of Prostitution in SM v. Croatia'. *International Labour Rights Case Law* 7:1 (2021): 74-79.

facilitates consistency across international frameworks and within the Convention framework.[121]

Other two applications considered in 2018 under Article 4 and found inadmissible illustrate that the Court is keeping firm the traditional approach to forced labour as not including work performed without payment. In Adigüzel v. Turkey,[122] the Court refused the application of a medical officer who had to perform work outside regular hours without financial compensation for about ten years. It emphasized that the applicant knew that his status required him to intervene outside working hours, during the night or even at weekends and should have known by embracing this profession that he could be called to issue the death certificate without additional payment. Therefore, the services at issue did not constitute 'forced or compulsory' work, which was imposed on the applicant against his will. The Court also pointed out that the applicant could take compensatory days off; this is why he could not claim to have been subject to a disproportionate burden.

This decision is easily placed in line with other decisions where the applicants believed that the lack of payment constituted the main factor of forced labour, but their opinion was not shared by the Court which reiterated that coercion is such factor.[123]

In the second case,[124] the obligations of the liquidator were at issue. The applicant claimed that the commercial court's failure to examine his request to be relieved of the liquidator's duties within a reasonable time caused him to remain the liquidator under threat of liability, which, for him, amounted to forced or compulsory labour. He submitted that the law required him to remain the bankrupt company's manager, a post which could not be ceased unilaterally. Considering the application the Court referred to its standards for evaluating what could be considered normal in respect of duties incumbent on members of a particular profession and would accordingly not be considered 'forced or compulsory labour'. It noted that the applicant's prior acceptance of appointment as a liquidator did not in itself warrant a conclusion that his situation cannot amount to forced or compulsory labour. The applicant, in the opinion of the Court, failed to clearly explain what particular work was required of him in the capacity of liquidator and to specify the exact reasons for which he wished to stop these activities. This is why the Court pointed out that the information provided by the applicant was wholly insufficient to assess the burden the impugned situation imposed on him and declared the application inadmissible. Yet, the Court's reasoning makes us assume that in a hypothetical case where the person will be able to demonstrate the disproportionate burden imposed by the delay in consideration of his application about the termination of liquidator's duties, the existence of forced labour might be established.

121. K. Hughes, 'Human Trafficking, SM v. Croatia and the Conceptual Evolution of Article 4 ECHR'. *The Modern Law Review* 85:4 (2022): 1044-1061.
122. ECtHR, ADIGÜZEL c. TURQUIE (7442/08) 06/02/2018.
123. Such as ECtHR, Vnuchko v. Ukraine (1198/04) 14/12/2006, Popov v. Ukraine (23892/03)14/12/2006, Sokur v. Ukraine (29439/02), 26/11/2002.
124. ECtHR, Barbarov v. Ukraine (75577/17) 27/03/2018.

In 2019, the Court considered another case against Greece about the lack of due protection for human trafficking victims.[125] Three Russian nationals arrived in Greece in 2003 after obtaining visas through the Consulate General of Greece in Moscow. They alleged that employees of the consulate had been bribed by Russian traffickers and had issued visas enabling them to be brought to Greece for the purposes of sexual exploitation. Women were recognized as 'victims of human trafficking' and the authorities instituted two sets of criminal proceedings against the persons suspected of exploiting them and in relation to the issuing of the visas.

Using the traditional framework for the analysis of this type of case, the court attached attention to the following factors: the existence of an appropriate legal and regulatory framework; operational measures taken to protect the applicants; the effectiveness of the police investigations and the judicial proceedings concerning the alleged exploitation and concerning the issuing of the visas.

The Court noticed that at the material time, there was appropriate legal and regulatory framework, as forced prostitution was classified as a lesser indictable offence, punishable by a prison term of between one and three years. This is why the time limits for the criminal proceeding were too short and the proceedings against two of the accused were terminated as being time-barred. It also observed that criminal proceedings had lasted for nine years for one of the applicants and were still suspended fifteen years after the complaint for another. These two applicants had therefore not had the benefit of an effective investigation and there had thus been a violation of the procedural aspect of Article 4. Consequently, the Court held that the competent authorities had not dealt with the case with the level of diligence required by Article 4 of the Convention and that the applicants had not been involved in the investigation to the extent required under the procedural limb of that provision.

In the course of 2021, the Court considered only one case[126] under Article 4 of the Convention. This case is of extreme importance since, for the first time, it concerned the trafficking of children and their engagement in illegal activities. The applicants, Vietnamese nationals and minors at the relevant time, were discovered by police to be working in cannabis factories and charged with being concerned with the production of a controlled drug. At the time, several national reports had found that Vietnamese children were particularly vulnerable to being trafficked into and within the United Kingdom and being exploited in such factories. The applicants were not referred immediately for assessment as potential victims of trafficking, but the Competent Authority later determined that both had been trafficked. The Crown Prosecution Service (CPS) disagreed with that assessment and pursued their prosecution. Both applicants pleaded guilty to the charges and were convicted.[127]

Only after conviction, the two minors were granted the status of victims of trafficking by the competent authority, but nevertheless, the CPS and also the Court of

125. ECtHR, T.I. and Others v. Greece (40311/10)18.07.2019.
126. ECtHR, CL. and A.N. v. United Kingdom, (77587/12 and 74603/12), 5.07.2021.
127. ECtHR, Legal summary. V.C.L. and A.N. v. the United Kingdom (77587/12, 74603/12) 16/02/2021, available at, https://hudoc.echr.coe.int/fre#{'itemid':['002-13143']}.

Appeal considered the reasons for the prosecution justified because of the extreme seriousness of the crimes, the absence of evidence of coercion and trafficking.

The two victims complained of infringement of Articles 4 and 6(1) of the Convention and Article 26 of the Anti-Trafficking Convention by the United Kingdom because they had been deprived of the protection to which they were entitled as victims of trafficking and because the State did not ensure identification and protection of victims, also non-criminalization of victims of trafficking for crimes committed related to status. Referring to the ILO Conventions on Forced Labour,[128] the Court proceeded to analyse the case in accordance with the provisions of Articles 4 and 6§1 of the Convention.

As a preliminary point, it reiterated that it is established that trafficking in human beings falls within the scope of Article 4 of the Convention[129] so it is not necessary to identify whether the treatment of which the applicant complains constitutes slavery, servitude or forced or compulsory labour.[130]

Given that at the time of the facts, there was sufficient evidence to give rise to the suspicion that the two applicants had been victims of trafficking, as well as that the English courts did not adequately justify the decision not to take into account the status of victims established by the competent authority, the Court concluded that the United Kingdom had not fulfilled the obligation to take operational measures to protect both initially - as a potential victim - and subsequently, as a person recognized by the competent authority victim of trafficking, thus violating Article 4 of the Convention.

Also, the ECtHR states that, although the status of victim does not automatically entail the right to criminal immunity and that the individual State remains free to prosecute or not the unlawful act, the States cannot underestimate the risk of double victimization of the person who suffers the trafficking, deriving from the fact of having to undergo criminal proceedings for unlawful acts that have been forced to do so as a victim of trafficking. They must therefore carry out certain preliminary assessments establishing the status of victim and, where appropriate, the link between the offence committed and the public interest in it being prosecuted.

This position of the Court deserves to be considered in more detail: it first stated that 'no general prohibition on the prosecution of victims of trafficking can be construed from the Anti-Trafficking Convention or any other international instrument' and that 'there is nothing in either instrument which could be interpreted as precluding the prosecution of child trafficking victims in all circumstances'. However, it states further, that such prosecution in certain circumstances, might be at odds with the State's duty to take operational measures to protect victims. This duty has two principal aims: to protect the victim of trafficking from further harm; and to facilitate his or her recovery. The Court then considered a non-punishment clause in light of the

128. In particular, Article 4 of the 2014 Protocol on Forced Labour, 1930 requires each Member State to take the necessary measures to ensure that the authorities *Can* not to prosecute or impose sanctions on victims of forced labour or obbleigatorio for their involvement in illegal activities that they are forced to commit as a direct consequence of being subjected to forced or compulsory labour.

129. *See* S.M. v. Croatia (60561/14), 25.06.2020, para. 296.

130. *See* Rantsev v. Cyprus and Russia (25964/04) 2010.

recovery aim. It stated: 'It is axiomatic that the prosecution of victims of trafficking would be injurious to their physical, psychological and social recovery and could potentially leave them vulnerable to being re-trafficked in future. Not only would they have to go through the ordeal of a criminal prosecution, but a criminal conviction could create an obstacle to their subsequent integration into society. In addition, incarceration may impede their access to the support and services that were envisaged by the Anti-Trafficking Convention' (paragraph 159). To avoid this, the Court emphasized the importance of early identification of a victim and underlined the need to use the criteria fixed in the Palermo Protocol and the Anti-Trafficking Convention (paragraph 160).

Summing up the position of the ECtHR, we can conclude that it was significantly influenced by Article 26 of the Anti-Trafficking Convention. Even though it did not state directly that the lack of non-punishment will constitute a violation of Article 4, it indirectly encouraged the states to ensure that the prosecution process takes into account the fact that the offence was committed by the victim of human trafficking. The ECtHR, in our opinion, could not go further than this, provided that even the norms of Article 26 of the Anti-Trafficking Convention 'leave a significant amount of discretion to states as to how they give effect to this'.[131] Also, if the Court has referred to the experience of the countries which have ratified the Anti-Trafficking Convention, it would have found that there is no 'European consensus' on the issue of non-punishment of the victims of human trafficking. As it was demonstrated in the GRETA report, 'of the 35 countries that had been evaluated, eight had adopted specific provisions on non-punishment, either in their criminal code or in anti-trafficking legislation. In four countries, the non-punishment provision applied to any trafficking-related offences. Its application was limited in three countries. Conversely, 27 countries did not have such measures in place. They relied rather on general provisions relating to duress, or else to exonerating or mitigating circumstances that were not specific to trafficked persons. In nine countries, the prosecution service had a discretion on whether to initiate a prosecution. Several countries had adopted guidelines on the application of the provision'.[132]

This case is a very important human rights contribution to the struggle with forced labour. As it was mentioned, both ILO Protocol No. 29 and the Council of Europe Convention on Action against Trafficking in Human Beings include a so-called non-punishment provision, which is an obligation of the states to provide for the possibility of not imposing penalties on victims for their involvement in unlawful activities, to the extent that they have been compelled to do so. The judgment should be read as encouraging the members of the CoE to consider the adoption of non-punishment norms as part of operational measures to protect the victims of human trafficking.

131. R. Piotrowicz and L. SorrentiNo. 'The Non-punishment Provision with Regard to Victims of Trafficking: A Human Rights Approach 1'. *Routledge Handbook of Human Trafficking*. Routledge. 2017, 171-184.

132. GRETA, 4th General Report on GRETA's Activities, March 2015, 52-54. Cited from R. Piotrowicz, and L. Sorrentino, 'The Non-punishment Provision with Regard to Victims of Trafficking: A Human Rights Approach 1'. *Routledge Handbook of Human Trafficking*. Routledge. 2017, 171-184.

Concluding this chapter, it should be noted that the Court in the period of the last five years had significantly broadened the scope of Article 4, including the exploitation through work and the exploitation of prostitution. It developed further the understanding of the States' obligation to identify and protect the victims of human trafficking, encouraging the members of the CoE to ensure that there is an opportunity for a 'non-punishment approach' to the offences committed by the victims of human trafficking. However, the Court still is not willing to include in the scope of protection under this article the cases when the applicants had to perform additional work without being paid.

CHAPTER 3

Prohibition of Discrimination

According to Article 14 of the ECHR, the enjoyment of the rights and freedoms *set out in the ECHR* should be secured without discrimination on any ground such as sex, race, colour, language, religion, political or other opinion, national or social origin, association with a national minority, property, birth or other status.

The open list of discriminatory grounds is a very important feature of the ECHR's approach to discrimination. It permitted the ECtHR to broaden the protection against discrimination beyond the classical list of protected characteristics adopted in many European countries and at the EU level. For example, the Court granted protection from discrimination against a child born out of wedlock[133] to people discriminated against on the grounds of their health[134] and because of the applicant's place of residence.[135]

It is also important to underline that the prohibition of Article 14 has a complementary nature, as it may be invoked and applied only together with other substantive guarantees of the Convention and its Protocols, which it complements.[136] The adoption of Protocol 12 to the ECHR[137] was intended to provide wider protection against discrimination without attaching the difference in treatment to the violation of ECHR rights. This Protocol contains a general prohibition of discrimination in the realization of any right guaranteed by law and might be more applicable in the sphere of labour rights' protection, as employment rights are not explicitly covered by the ECHR. According to the ECtHR, the same standards developed under Article 14 are applicable to cases brought under Article 1 of Protocol No. 12.[138] However, it has, as of the date

133. In respect of inheritance rights, *see*, e.g., ECtHR, Quilichini v. France (38299/15) 14/03/2019.
134. ECtHR, Novruk and Others v. Russia (31039/11, 48511/11, 76810/12, 14618/13 and 13817/14) 15.03.2016; Kiyutin v. Russia (2700/10) 10/03/2011.
135. ECtHR, Pichkur v. Ukraine (10441/06) 7 November 2013.
136. E. Villiger, 'Prohibition of Discrimination (Article 14 of the Convention)'. *Handbook on the European Convention on Human Rights*. Brill Nijhoff. 2022, 580-591.
137. Signed in Rome on 5 November 2000.
138. ECtHR, Moraru and Marin v. Romania (53282/18 31428/20) 20/12/2022, para. 100.

of writing, been ratified by only twenty states[139] (out of the forty-six members of the CoE).

Before considering the most recent case law on Article 14 and Protocol No. 12, there is a need to briefly outline the key features of the system of protection from discrimination elaborated by the Court. The ECtHR established the criteria to understand if a given difference in treatment contravened Article 14. It held that 'the principle of equality of treatment is violated if the distinction has no objective and reasonable justification'.[140] The existence of such justification must be assessed in relation to the aim of the impugned measure, having regard to the principles which normally prevail in democratic societies. A difference of treatment in the exercise of a right laid down by the Convention must not only pursue a legitimate aim: Article 14 will also be violated when it is clearly established that there is no reasonable relationship of proportionality between the means employed and the aim sought to be realized.[141]

Therefore, the ECtHR's consideration of discrimination cases includes several main steps: the establishment of the difference in treatment, of an 'objective and reasonable justification' for discriminatory provisions or treatment in the form of a legitimate aim and, finally, if there had been proportionality between 'the means employed and the aim sought to be realized'.[142]

The burden of proof in discrimination cases is distributed in the following way: once the applicant has shown a difference in treatment between persons in relevantly similar situations, it is for the Government to show that it was justified.[143] A difference in treatment may take the form of disproportionately prejudicial effects of a general policy or measure which, though couched in neutral terms, discriminates against a group. Such a situation may amount to indirect discrimination, which does not necessarily require discriminatory intent.[144] In cases concerning indirect discrimination, the ECtHR held that the burden of proof should shift to the respondent State if the applicant establishes the rebuttable presumption that the effect of a measure or practice had been discriminatory.[145] It also noted that it would be extremely difficult in practice for applicants to prove indirect discrimination without such a shift.[146]

In considering whether a relevant difference in treatment existed, the ECtHR considers the treatment of persons in analogous, or relevantly similar, situations. The requirement to demonstrate an analogous position does not require that the comparator groups be identical, but an applicant must demonstrate that, having regard to the particular nature of his or her complaint, he or she was in a relevantly similar situation to others treated differently.[147]

139. The status of the Protocol No. 12 to the ECHR. Available at, onventions.coe.int/Treaty/Commun/ChercheSig.asp?NT = 177&CM = &DF = &CL = ENG (accessed 23 January 2023).
140. *See* Fábián v. Hungary (78117/13) GC 05/09/2017.
141. ECtHR, B. v. Switzerland 78630/12 20/10/2020, para. 62.
142. ECtHR, Belli and Arquier-Martinez v. Switzerland (65550/, 11/12/2018), para. 90.
143. ECtHR, Savickis and Others v. Latvia (49270/11) 09/06/2022, para. 187.
144. ECtHR, P.C. v. IRELAND (26922/19) 01/09/2022.
145. ECtHR, Horváth and Kiss v. Hungary (11146/11) 29 January 2013, para. 108.
146. *Ibid.*
147. ECtHR, Fábián v. Hungary (78117/13) GC 05/09/2017, para. 113.

Throughout the ECHR's history, a great variety of labour-related cases was considered under Article 14. There were cases of unfair dismissal,[148] suspension from work,[149] the lack of the right for paternity leave[150] or difference in the amount of damages received in case of occupational injury or illness,[151] etc. Application about the dismissals was considered due to the living interpretation of Article 8 of the Convention, which guarantees respect for private and family life.[152] The demonstrated in Chapter 1 inclusion of the right to develop relations with others (also of a professional nature) has become the 'magic gate' for those who bring cases about unfair dismissal before the ECtHR. The dismissal, in the opinion of the Court, affects this right and, therefore, might be considered a violation of the negative obligations of the states under ECHR, if the applicant was employed by the State. The violation of positive obligations of the States to secure the rights under ECHR to those within their jurisdiction[153] might be found if the applicant was dismissed by a private company and the States did not ensure due protection of the convention rights in domestic proceedings.

In the last five years, the Court also considered several cases under Article 14 and Protocol No. 12 of the ECHR. In particular, in 2017, it considered the case relevant to occupational health. In Saumier v. France,[154] the applicant contracted an occupational illness which left her severely disabled as a result of an inexcusable negligence by her employer. Under French law, liability for work-related accidents or occupational disease is governed by a special set of rules, which, irrespective of any liability on the part of the employer, are based on automatic cover by the health insurance fund and the maximum sum is specified. The applicant argued that she should be entitled to full compensation as an individual who had suffered damage occurring in a different context. Therefore, the Court had to determine if there was a difference in treatment establishing if the employees who had an occupational disease as a result of negligence by their employer were in an analogous or comparable situation to that of individuals who had sustained damage to health as a result of negligence by a third party. It stated that the situation of employees was a special one because there is a contractual relationship and subordination, this is why there are special rules of civil liability which are not based on proof of negligence, a causal link between that negligence and the damage but on solidarity and automaticity. Thus, the state ensured that the compensation was automatic, speedy and secure. The reference to the system of payment of compensation as a special one envisaged only for occupational illnesses and injuries made the court decide that different sets of legal rules applied to persons in different situations. ECtHR concluded that in the absence of difference in treatment, there was

148. ECtHR, Emel Boyraz v. Turkey (61960/08) 2 December 2014.
149. ECtHR, Eweida and others v. The United Kingdom (N 48420/10) 15 January 2013.
150. ECtHR, Markin Konstantin v. Russia (No. 30078/06) Grand Chamber, 22 March 2012.
151. ECtHR, Saumier v. France (74734/14) 12/01/2017.
152. ECtHR, Emel Boyraz v. Turkey, Hülya Ebru Demirel v. Turkey (30733/08) 19 June 2018.
153. ECtHR, Eweida and Others v. The United Kingdom (48420/10 36516/10 51671/10) 15/01/2013, para. 83.
154. ECtHR, Saumier v. France (74734/14) 12/01/2017.

no discrimination and no violation of Article 14 taken in conjunction with Article 1 of Protocol No. 1.

We suppose that this case is an example of the very wide margin of appreciation left to the states under Article 14. The Court has numerously stated that the extent of this margin of appreciation varies according to circumstances, fields and context and that it is usually wide when general economic or social measures are concerned.[155] The Court in such cases 'will in principle respect the State's conception of the requirements of the public interest, unless its judgment proves to be "manifestly lacking in reasonableness"'.[156]

At the same time, in the cases about the difference of treatment based on gender, the Court stated that the margin of appreciation of the States is very narrow.[157] In such situations, the principle of proportionality does not merely require that the measure chosen should in general be suited to the fulfilment of the aim pursued, but it must also be shown that it was necessary in the circumstances of the case.[158] In 2018, the Court had an opportunity to develop this stance in a case about the dismissal of a woman for being a woman. The case Hülya Ebru Demirel v. Turkey concerned the refusal to employ a woman as a security officer and her further dismissal because she did not fulfil the requirements of 'being a man' and 'having completed military service'.[159] The applicant challenged the refusal in domestic court and was hired after the court of first instance gave the state of execution to the employer's decision not to hire her and later ruled in her favour. The employer made an appeal and asked the second-instance court to issue the state of execution of the first-instance court's judgment. The appellate court granted the employer's application and the woman was dismissed from her post.

Bringing the claim before the ECtHR the applicant asserted the violation of Article 14 (prohibition of discrimination) and of Article 11 of the Convention on the Elimination of All Forms of Discrimination against Women ('the CEDAW'), which prohibits discrimination against women in the field of employment. The Court considered the claim in light of Articles 8 and 14 of the ECHR.

This case is very similar to Emel Boyraz v. Turkey, considered by the ECtHR in 2014, with the only exception that the refusal to hire a woman was not considered a violation of the ECHR in that case. Emel Boyraz was also terminated from her job as she did not fulfil the requirements of 'being a man' and 'having completed military service'. The respondent stated that the post in question had been reserved for male candidates in view of the nature of the service and the need to recruit male personnel. The ECtHR accepted that there may be legitimate requirements for certain occupational activities depending on their nature or the context in which they are carried out. However, the mere fact that security officers had to work night shifts and in rural areas and might be required to use firearms and physical force did not, the Court found, in itself justify the

155. ECtHR, Carson and others v. UK [GC] (42184/05) 16 March 2010, para. 61; Saumier v. France (74734/14) 12/01/2017, para. 51.
156. *Ibid.*
157. ECtHR, Emel Boyraz v. Turkey (61960/08) 2 December 2014; Markin Konstantin v. Russia (No. 30078/06) Grand Chamber, 22 March 2012.
158. ECtHR, Emel Boyraz v. Turkey (61960/08) 2 December 2014, para. 51.
159. ECtHR, Hülya Ebru Demirel v. Turkey (30733/08) 19 June 2018, para. 9.

difference in treatment between men and women in this way. In the ECtHR's view, only the personal inability of the applicant to fulfil these tasks might be the legitimate reason for dismissal.[160] The ECtHR is particularly rigorous in its approach to the justification of discrimination based on gender, or sexual orientation.

In neither of the cases, the Government provided arguments on the necessity of a discriminatory measure. Instead, the State submitted that the norms of the ECHR are not applicable in the case as it concerned a right which was not secured by the Convention, namely the right to recruitment as a public servant (in Demirel v. Turkey, they referred to the absence of the right to access a particular profession).

In the Boyraz case, the Court noted that indeed the right of recruitment to the civil service was deliberately omitted from the Convention.[161] But it considered that the applicant should be regarded as an official who was appointed to the civil service and subsequently dismissed and found the violation of both Articles 8 and 14 of the ECHR.[162]

Hence, four years later when the Court considered Demirel v. Turkey case, there were already grounds to consider the case about the dismissal on discriminatory grounds in light of ECHR. However, it is not clear enough how to justify the consideration of a refusal to be hired in a particular position under Article 8. The Court skipped this difficulty, having decided that the case is identical to Emel Boyraz. 'For the detailed reasons elaborated on in Emel Boyraz'[163] it concluded that there has been a violation of Article 14 taken in conjunction with Article 8 resulting from the refusal of the authorities to appoint, and then their subsequent dismissal of the applicant from the post of a security officer. It remains questionable if the refusal to be employed might constitute a separate violation of Articles 8 and 14 as the part of the judgment where the refusal to hire the applicant was found to be in violation of the ECHR remained without reasoning.[164] The hypothetical reasoning might also engage Article 3 prohibiting degrading treatment. The Court might also further develop the dignity-based understanding of the right to respect to private life, granted by Article 8. Roots might be found for that in already acknowledged right to personal development, and the right to establish and develop relationships with other human beings and the outside world.[165] Perhaps this opportunity has seemed far too activist even for ECtHR, which is already famous for its judicial activism.

Even though no reasons are provided for considering a discriminatory refusal to hire a woman as a violation of Article 8, this judgment is a significant step towards

160. ECtHR, Emel Boyraz v. Turkey (61960/08) 2/12/2014.
161. Emel Boyraz v. Turkey, para. 41.
162. One year earlier in Volkov v. Ukraine (Oleksandr Volkov v. Ukraine (21722/11) 09/01/2013), unfair dismissal of a judge was found to be in breach of the right to respect of private life with the result that the State was obliged to ensure the applicant's reinstatement.
163. *Ibid.*, para. 35.
164. *See* comments of A. Timmer, Of Firearms and Weak Women: Sex Discrimination in Hülya Ebru Demirel v. Turkey, 31.07.2018, http://strasbourgobservers.com/2018/07/31/of-firearms-and-weak-women-sex-discrimination-in-hulya-ebru-demirel-v-turkey/#more-4206 (accessed 20 February 2019).
165. ECtHR, Niemietz v. Germany (13710/88) 16/12/1992, para. 29; Oleksandr Volkov v. Ukraine, paras 165-167.

establishing equality in the labour market. Prohibitions to employ women in certain occupations or professions still exist in a number of countries, for example, Belarus, Azerbaijan, Tajikistan, Turkmenistan, and Kyrgyzstan.[166] In Ukraine, Georgia and Armenia these lists were only recently repealed.[167] The present judgment is a gest of support for women struggling for equal rights, it demonstrates the unanimity of international bodies finding that norms prohibiting women from certain employment violate their human rights.[168]

Two years later, however, considering another case, the Court seems to have stepped from its conviction of a state's narrow margin of appreciation in cases of gender discrimination. In 2020, the Court considered Napotnik v. Romania[169] case under Protocol No. 12 to the ECHR. The applicant argued that her recalling from a diplomatic post abroad after announcing pregnancy was discriminatory. This case is an interesting, rare and rather debatable example of the finding that difference in treatment based on sex was justified.

The applicant had a four-year post as a consular officer at the Romanian embassy in Ljubljana, which started in 2007. In April 2007, she married a Slovenian official and a few months later she became pregnant with their first child. During pregnancy, she was often absent from work for a few days because of health problems linked to her pregnancy. In the periods of her absence, the ambassador asked for a replacement, but no person was sent. The consular section was closed during the applicant's absence and requests for assistance were redirected to other embassies. In a separate communication sent to the Ministry of Foreign Affairs by the ambassador, it was stated that the applicant 'was of little use to the diplomatic mission in Ljubljana' (paragraph 23). By a ministerial order of 20 January 2009, the applicant's posting to Ljubljana was terminated and she was expected to return to the Bucharest office on 14 February 2009.

The Government argued that the decision to recall the applicant from her posting abroad had pursued the legitimate aim of the protection of the rights of others, notably Romanian nationals in need of consular assistance in Slovenia (paragraph 79). The Court accepted this aim. Considering the proportionality of the measure, it noted that the applicant's absence from the office seriously affected consular activity in the embassy (paragraph 80). It further underlined that she was not dismissed and recalling was not a disciplinary measure and was not intended to put her in an unfavourable position. She even continued to be promoted by her employer. On these arguments, the Court based its conclusion that 'the early termination of the applicant's diplomatic posting abroad was necessary for ensuring and maintaining the functional capacity of the diplomatic mission, and ultimately the protection of the rights of others'.[170]

166. Professions Prohibited to Women: Gender Discrimination Human Rights Report of the ADC 'Memorial'. March 2018. Available at, https://adcmemorial.org/wp-content/uploads/forbidden_2018RUwww.pdf (accessed 20 December 2022).
167. *Ibid.*
168. Opinion of the UN CEDW No. 60/2013, 21 March 2016; UN CEDAW. Concluding observations to the 3-4 periodic reports of Kazakhstan. CEDAW / C / KAZ / CO / 3-4. 3 October 2014.
169. ECtHR, Napotnik v. Romania (33139/13) 20.10.2020.
170. *Ibid.*, para. 86.

Surprisingly, the Court did not consider the fact that the office was closed because the Ministry did not send anyone to substitute the applicant as it was requested by the Ambassador. Neither is it considered that before 2006 the work of the applicant was performed by people working under temporary contracts. The Court did not consider that the Government had other options to ensure maintaining the functional capacity of the diplomatic mission. Thus, instead of granting a traditional narrow margin of appreciation to the state in cases of gender discrimination, the margin left to Romania, in this case, was far too broad.

The Court cited the norms of other international and EU instruments but came to the conclusions which, in our opinion, are contrary to EU Directive 2006/54/EC of the European Parliament and of the Council of 5 July 2006 on the implementation of the principle of equal opportunities and equal treatment of men and women in matters of employment and occupation. Under Article 15 of this Directive, a woman on maternity leave shall be entitled, after the end of her period of maternity leave, to return to her job or to an equivalent post on terms and conditions which are no less favourable to her and to benefit from any improvement in working conditions to which she would have been entitled during her absence. It definitely means that the place of work should be the same, in particular, when the need to transfer to another country is at stake.

Interestingly, the Court did not refer to the ILO Conventions Nos 111 and 183, which were ratified by Romania and, therefore, constitute part of its legal order. Convention No. 111 defines discrimination and also clarifies what should not be deemed discrimination: (a) the term includes any distinction, exclusion or preference made on the basis of race, colour, sex, religion, political opinion, national extraction or social origin, *which has the effect of nullifying or impairing equality* of opportunity or treatment in employment or occupation; (b) such other distinction, exclusion or preference which has the effect of nullifying or impairing equality of opportunity or treatment in employment or occupation as may be determined by the Member concerned after consultation with representative employers' and workers' organizations, where such exist, and with other appropriate bodies.

Let's recall, that the Court in the concluding paragraphs of the judgment underlined that the recalling from post 'was not intended to put her in an unfavourable position'. Even if there was no such intent, the changes to her job condition definitely had *the effect of nullifying or impairing equality* of treatment, as she would not have been recalled if she was not pregnant. Further, ILO Convention No. 111 states that any distinction, exclusion or preference in respect of a particular job based on the inherent requirements thereof shall not be deemed to be discrimination. There are strong doubts that the requirement to be always available and not take maternity or medical leaves might be considered an inherent requirement to the job of the consular officer. Also, Romania has ratified ILO Convention No. 183. Under Article 8(2), a woman is guaranteed the right to return to the same position or an equivalent position paid at the same rate at the end of her maternity leave. The reference to these norms, in our opinion, might have inclined the Court to a different conclusion. We believe that permitting crucial changes in the working conditions of a woman because of pregnancy is a dangerous step. In a way, many job positions might be considered necessary and engaged in 'the protection of the rights of others'. Employers should not have the discretion to substitute such workers or to get rid of them in this position in case of an employee's pregnancy or maternity leave.

In 2012, the ECtHR considered a case on gender discrimination in the entitlement to paternity leaves – Gruba and Others v. Russia – which united four applications of policemen.[171] It should be mentioned that the applicants were presented before the Court by Konstantin Markin, who since the famous case has received legal education and the status of a lawyer. Under Russian law, male police officers were entitled to parental leave only if their children were left without maternal care (in case of the mother's death, withdrawal of parental authority, lengthy illness, etc.). Even though the wives of two applicants had health problems and were recommended not to lift any objects exceeding 5 kg, they still were considered able to take care of children. The applicants argued that the difference in entitlement to parental leave between policemen and policewomen violates the ECHR. The Court held the difference in entitlement to parental leave had not been justified, and that the authorities had failed to balance the legitimate aim of operational effectiveness of the police and the applicants' rights not to be discriminated against on grounds of gender. In conclusion, it found the violation of Article 14 in conjunction with Article 8. The commentators noted that the Court must be applauded for continuing further upon the path previously taken in Markin, by condemning gender stereotypes surrounding care and paid work.[172] Unfortunately, from the point of view of a Russian lawyer, this judgment is not capable of challenging the way of things as even the changes to the legislation which should have been brought after the Markin case were never adopted (although proposed before the Duma). On 16 September 2022, Russia ceased to be a Party to the ECHR, and in current circumstances, there is almost no chance that this judgment will be enforced. According to the information received from K. Markin, the courts in Russia refused to reopen the cases even though under the Russian Civil Procedure Code, the adoption of judgment by the ECtHR is a ground for the reopening of proceedings.

Finally, in 2021, the convention norms on the prohibition of discrimination were referred to in the applications for special anti-COVID measures adopted at workplaces. In particular, the application of Mr Thevenon against France which was communicated to the respondent state in 2021 and has been declared inadmissible in October 2022. Relying on Article 8, Article 14 and Article 1 of Protocol No. 1 (protection of property), the applicant complained of the vaccination requirement imposed on him under French Law as his profession – a firefighter – was on the list of those, where the vaccination is compulsory unless there was a medical exemption. His refusal to be vaccinated led to his suspension from work and the complete loss of his pay.[173] The application was found inadmissible because of the non-exhaustion of domestic remedies by the applicant. The Court still referred to several decisions of the French Conseil

171. ECtHR, Gruba and Others v. Russia (66180/09, 30771/11, 50089/11 and 22165/12) 06.07.2021.
172. Alicia Hendricks, Gruba and Others v. Russia: The ECtHR Repeats Its Konstantin Markin v. Russia Jurisprudence But (Again) Misses A Child-Oriented Perspective. 1 October 2021, https://strasbourgobservers.com/2021/10/01/gruba-and-others-v-russia-the-ecthr-repeats-its-konstantin-markin-v-russia-jurisprudence-but-again-misses-a-child-oriented-perspective/.
173. ECtHR, Thevenon v. France (dec.) (46061/21) 13/09/2022.

d'Etat which found the new norms on compulsory vaccination lawful, considering them also in light of the ECHR.

Article 14 was referred to in the applications against Greece, lodged by thirty health professionals who work independently or in public health institutions. They complain about the law which imposes compulsory vaccination of health-sector professionals against COVID-19 as a condition for being able to continue exercising their occupation. The applicants requested that the Court apply interim measures to suspend immediately the application of the law, but the Court decided to reject the requests for interim measures, holding that they were outside the scope of Rule 39 (interim measures). These measures might be granted only on an exceptional basis when the applicants would otherwise face a real risk of irreversible harm.[174] The same reasoning might be found in the decision to reject the requests for interim measures in the case Abgrall et 671 others v. France,[175] brought by French firefighters under Articles 2 and 8 of the ECHR about the suspension from work for the refusal to undergo compulsory vaccination.[176]

Also, under Article 14 of the ECHR, the Court received the application on the management of the public health crisis caused by COVID-19 in France. Relying on Articles 3, 8 and 14 of the Convention and Article 1 of Protocol No. 12, the applicant stated that the laws which created and imposed a health pass system amounted to discriminatory interference with the right to respect for private life and were intended primarily to coerce individuals into consenting to vaccination.[177] The Court did consider the application on merits having found that the applicant did not exhaust domestic remedies and abused *the right of application* (*Article 35-3-a of the ECHR*). Mr Zambrano created a mechanism to submit multiple applications to the ECtHR through an automatically generated and standardized application form and almost 18,000 were submitted as a result of this technique. Having analysed the texts at the site of the applicant and his videos, the Court established that the applicant pursued the aim to bring about 'congestion, excessive workload and a backlog' at the Court, to 'derail the system', he also stated that 'paralyzing the functioning of the European Court of Human Rights will send a strong and clear message, not only to the French government but to all European governments'.[178] The Court also underlined that the application lacked legal arguments.

The consideration of these cases brings us to the idea that the applications alleging that the obligatory COVID vaccination for some workers amounted to a violation of the ECHR are in the majority rather emotional than well-articulated. They do lack substantive legal reasoning and compliance with the requirement to exhaust domestic remedies.

174. ECtHR, Press release. Refusal of requests for interim measures in respect of the Greek law on compulsory vaccination of health-sector staff against COVID-19. 9 September 2021.
175. The application No. 41950/21, Abgrall et 671 autres c. France.
176. ECtHR, Les demandes de mesures provisoires de 672 sapeurs-pompiers concernant la loi relative à la gestion de la crise sanitaire n'entrent pas dans le champ d'application de l'article 39 du règlement de la Cour. CEDH 243 (2021) 25.08.2021.
177. ECtHR, Zambrano v. France (dec.) (41994/21) 21/09/2021.
178. *Ibid.*, para. 11.

The approach of the ECtHR to the compulsory vaccination of workers might be deduced from its reasoning in Vavřička and Others v. the Czech Republic on the obligatory vaccination of pupils considered under Article 8.[179] To make the COVID narrative of this book more consistent, this case will be considered in this part. The application was lodged several years before the COVID pandemic, but the judgment was delivered during it. We suppose that the judges provided very elaborate reasoning for the absence of violation and also had in mind the COVID measures when writing about other types of vaccination. COVID was also referred to in the *submission of the third-party interveners, in particular, of the French government.*[180] The applicants alleged that the various consequences for them of non-compliance with the statutory duty of vaccination had been incompatible with their right to respect for their private life under Article 8 of the Convention. Some also complained under Article 9 of the Convention and Article 2 of Protocol No. 1. Some of the points of the Court's reasoning, in this case, had direct relevance to the compulsory vaccination of workers: first, it acknowledged that compulsory vaccination, as an involuntary medical intervention, represents an interference with the right to respect for private life within the meaning of Article 8 of the Convention.[181] To determine whether this interference entailed a violation of Article 8 of the Convention, the Court examined if the vaccination was 'in accordance with the law', pursued one or more of the legitimate aims specified therein, and was proportionate to the aim pursued. It referred to numerous international acts, the opinion of the WHO, and the practice of other European states and formulated the following important legal positions justifying compulsory vaccination:

- a general consensus existed among the Contracting Parties, strongly supported by international specialized bodies, that vaccination was one of the most successful and cost-effective health interventions and that each State should aim to achieve the highest possible level of vaccination;
- healthcare policy matters came within the margin of appreciation of the national authorities who were best placed to assess priorities and social needs;
- compulsory vaccination is not an absolute duty as an exemption from the duty is permitted notably in respect of children with a permanent contraindication to vaccination;
- there is no provision allowing for vaccination to be forcibly administered;
- the procedural safeguards were provided for in domestic law;
- there is a general consensus over the vital importance of this means of protecting populations against diseases that may have severe effects on individual health, and that, in the case of serious outbreaks, may cause disruption to society;
- the safety of the vaccines in use remains under continuous monitoring by the competent authorities.[182]

179. ECtHR, Vavřička and Others v. the Czech Republic [GC] (47621/13 3867/14 73094/14) 08/04/2021.
180. *Ibid.*, paras 210 and 212.
181. ECtHR, Solomakhin v. Ukraine (24429/03) 15 March 2012, para. 33.
182. ECtHR, Vavřička and Others v. the Czech Republic, paras 290-307.

It might be presumed that the majority of COVID measures imposed at the workplaces and the compulsory vaccination of some workers in the countries of the Council of Europe corresponded to the requirements formulated by the Court in Vavřička and Others v. the Czech Republic. Although it has to be decided on a case-by-case basis, compulsory vaccination per se would not violate these fundamental rights; however, sanctions related to the refusal of vaccination may rise proportionality questions.[183] The scholars note that compulsory vaccination is conceivable for diseases that are particularly contagious and associated with considerable risks while the vaccine offered is safe and effective.[184]

Summing up the results of the research provided in this chapter we would like to underscore that in the last five years the jurisprudence of the ECtHR on Article 14 in cases related to employment provided some novelty. It can be described as broadening the scope of protection against gender discrimination in access to employment (*see* Demirel v. Turkey) but surprisingly limiting it when the pregnancy-related changes to the employment conditions of women are concerned (*see* Napotnik v. Romania). The Court remains open to considering cases of discrimination on grounds not explicitly listed in Article 14 (*see* Saumier v. France). This openness is very important in cases when particular grounds of discrimination are not recognized by national or EU law.[185]

183. S. Hungler, 'Compulsory Vaccination and Fundamental Human Rights in the World of Work'. *Studia Iuridica Lublinensia* 31:1 (2022): 63-77.
184. A. Krasser, 'Compulsory Vaccination in a Fundamental Rights Perspective: Lessons from the ECtHR'. *ICL Journal* 15:2 (2021): 207-233. https://doi.org/10.1515/icl-2021-0010.
185. *See*, e.g., C.B. Olsen, 'When Mandatory Exercise at Work Meets Employees' Rights to Privacy and Non-discrimination: A Comparative and European Perspective'. *European Labour Law Journal* 12:3 (2021): 338-362.

Chapter 4

Employee's Right to Respect for Private Life

> ARTICLE 8 Right to respect for private and family life 1. Everyone has the right to respect for his private and family life, his home and his correspondence. 2. There shall be no interference by a public authority with the exercise of this right except such as is in accordance with the law and is necessary in a democratic society in the interests of national security, public safety or the economic well-being of the country, for the prevention of disorder or crime, for the protection of health or morals, or for the protection of the rights and freedoms of others.

In Chapter 1, we have already demonstrated some examples of the broadening of the scope of Article 8. The Court has stated in many judgments since 2009 that Article 8 should guarantee 'privacy' in the broadest sense of the term, which includes the right to a 'private social life', i.e., the possibility for the individual to develop his/her social identity, enshrining 'the possibility to reach out to others in order to establish and develop relationships with fellow human beings'.[186] Also, it held that the restrictions on an individual's professional life may fall within Article 8 where they have repercussions on the manner in which he or she constructs his or her social identity by developing relationships with others in the course of their working life and that the majority of people have a significant, if not the greatest, opportunity to develop relationships with the outside world.[187]

Article 8 protects the human right to privacy at the workplace (encompassing privacy of correspondence,[188] e-mail use,[189] of the offices in some circumstances,[190] data protection,[191] access to data,[192] professional reputation[193]) and provides the

186. ECtHR, Bigaeva v. Greece (26713/05) 28/05/2009, para. 22.
187. ECtHR, Bărbulescu v. Romania (61496/08) GC 05/09/2017.
188. *Ibid.*
189. ECtHR, Copland v. the United Kingdom (62617/00) 3 April 2007.
190. ECtHR, Peev v. Bulgaria (64209/01) 26 July 2007.
191. ECtHR, Surikov v. Ukraine (No. 42788/06) 26.01.2017; López Ribalda and Others v. Spain [GC] (1874/13 8567/13) 17/10/2019.

grounds for protection in cases of unfair dismissals[194] or transfers to different work[195] if it violated the right to develop relationships with others, deduced from this article in the Court's case law. In this chapter, we will deal with these two groups of cases, starting with the consideration of the requirements that might justify the interference with the right to privacy under paragraph 2 of Article 8.

4.1 PROTECTION OF AN EMPLOYEE'S PRIVACY UNDER ARTICLE 8 OF THE ECHR: GENERAL FRAMEWORK

The introduction of a framework for considering cases on employees' privacy and the proposal of a 'checklist' of questions to be responded to by national courts[196] in similar cases are the key achievements of the ECtHR. This framework is deduced from the second paragraph of Article 8 and complimented with the 'reasonableness of the expectations of privacy' test applied in the majority of workplace privacy cases. Thus, considering such cases, the Court first (but not always) establishes if the employee had a reasonable expectation of privacy,[197] then the ECtHR considers if there had been an interference with the right to privacy and evaluates its lawfulness and necessity.[198] The proportionality assessment of the interference with the legitimate aim pursued by the employer is the most important part of the last step.[199]

This framework is applicable in case of the violation of the states' negative obligation not to interfere with the right to privacy, when the case is brought, for example, by a public servant.[200] Also, it is used in the cases on positive obligations of the states to secure the right to privacy in relations between private parties, involving also the obligations of national courts to correctly considered the case in line with Article 8.[201] While Article 8 contains no explicit procedural requirements, the decision-making process involved in measures of interference with this right must be fair and ensure due respect for the interests safeguarded by Article 8.[202]

192. ECtHR, Yonchev v. Bulgaria (No. 12504/09) 07.12.2017.
193. ECtHR, S.W. v. The United Kingdom (87/18) 22/06/2021.
194. ECtHR, Hülya Ebru Demirel v. Turkey (30733/08) 19 June 2018, ECtHR, Denisov v. Ukraine (76639/11) GC, 25 September 2018.
195. ECtHR, Sodan c. Turquie (18650/05) 02/02/2016.
196. *See*, in particular, such a list in ECtHR, Bărbulescu v. Romania (61496/08)GC 05/09/2017, para. 121.
197. *See*, e.g., ECtHR, Halford v. United Kingdom (20605/92) 25/07/1997, para. 44 and Copland v. the United Kingdom (62617/00) 03/04/2007, para. 42.
198. ECtHR, Halford v. United Kingdom (20605/92) 25/07/1997; Copland v. the United Kingdom (62617/00) 03/04/2007; ECtHR, Peev v. Bulgary, para. 43.
199. ECtHR, Halford v. United Kingdom (20605/92) 25/07/1997; Copland v. the United Kingdom (62617/00) 03/04/2007; ECtHR, Peev v. Bulgary, para. 43.
200. ECtHR, Pay v. UK (32792/05) inadmissible 16 September 2008, or Peev v. Bulgaria (64209/01) 26 July 2007, Radu v. Moldova (50073/07) 15 April 2014.
201. ECtHR, Köpke v. Germany (420/07) inadmissible 05/10/2010; Bărbulescu v. Romania (61496/08) 12/01/2016.
202. ECtHR, Guide on Article 8 of the Convention: Right to Respect for Private and Family Life. Updated on 31 August 2022.

Reasonableness of the Expectations of Privacy

The concept of a 'reasonable expectation of privacy' came to Strasbourg jurisprudence from the United States of America (USA). It was developed in privacy cases considered under the Fourth Amendment to the US Constitution, which protects its citizens from unreasonable searches and seizures of their persons, houses and belongings which might be carried out by the government. In 1967, US Justice John Marshall Harlan suggested a test for 'reasonable expectation of privacy' in Katz v. United States. He proposed two standards by which it could be determined whether a person had a reasonable expectation of privacy. First, a person must have had an actual (subjective) expectation of privacy in the given situation. Second, society more broadly would accept this expectation as being reasonable (i.e., the objective counterpart).[203]

Recent research has found that out of around 8,000 judgments, decisions, advisory opinions, reports and resolutions on Article 8 ECHR, only in about twenty of those was the term 'reasonable expectation of privacy' used by the Court and mostly in cases in the workplace privacy.[204] Interestingly, in the cases considered in the last five years, the Court tends to only cite this concept, without building the main legal positions on it. It numerously stated that 'the reasonable expectations as to privacy may be a significant, although not necessarily conclusive, factor' in the assessment of the interference with the right to privacy under Article 8.[205] This position has been expressed in the cases of employees monitoring through special technologies: video and e-mail monitoring. In the Bărbulescu case, the employee had signed a document prohibiting the use of employers' devices and the Internet for personal purposes. Still, the Court concluded that 'employer's instructions cannot reduce private social life in the workplace to zero' and that 'respect for private life and for the privacy of correspondence continues to exist, even if these may be restricted in so far as necessary'.[206] In other words, the presence of employer's regulations on monitoring and the employee's consent on the use of different technologies for the control of his/her working activities does not per se legitimize these control measures. Presumably, the use of the new technologies made the Court reluctant to rely on the concept of the reasonableness of the expectations of privacy in the most recent case law on workplace privacy. In Libert v. France,[207] for example, the case on the access of an employer to the files stored on the applicant's working computer, this concept was not mentioned at all. As correctly pointed out by Joe Atkinson, the use of reasonable expectations as the touchstone for Article 8 engagement is problematic in societies

203. S. Nouwt and B.R. de Vries, 'Introduction', in: Sjaak Nouwt, Berend R. de Vries, Corien Prins, (eds) *Reasonable Expectations of Privacy? Eleven Country Reports on Camera Surveillance and Workplace Privacy*. Cambridge University Press. 2005, 3.
204. B. van der Sloot, 'Expectations of Privacy: The Three Tests Deployed by the European Court of Human Rights' in: Dara Hallinan, Ronald Leenes, Paul De Hert (eds) *Data Protection and Privacy, Enforcing Rights in a Changing World*, Bloomsbury Publishing. 2021, 73.
205. ECtHR, Bărbulescu, para. 73; Antović and Mirković v. Montenegro (70838/13) 28.11.2017, para. 43.
206. ECtHR, Bărbulescu, para. 81.
207. ECtHR, Libert v. France (application No. 588/13) 22.02.2018.

where intrusive technologies are prevalent, or surveillance is widespread.[208] Evidently, with the development of digital technologies of surveillance and the spread of distant work, the reliance on the classical test of the reasonable expectation of privacy might lead to the denial of this right in practice. Therefore, nowadays, the attention to the necessity and proportionality of the interference based on the consideration of particular circumstances of each case becomes of crucial importance for the ECtHR. The same approach should be followed by the national courts as well.

'In Accordance with the Law'

The ECtHR had stated that the phrase 'in accordance with the law' requires, at a minimum, compliance with domestic law.[209] The quality of that law is also relevant.[210] It should be foreseeable and sufficiently clear in its terms to give individuals an adequate indication as to the circumstances in which and the conditions on which the State would be entitled to resort to measures affecting those rights.[211] In the view of the ECtHR in order to find the interference to be in accordance with law, the law in question should be accessible to the individual concerned[212] and be clearly formulated.[213] In Antunes Rocha v. Portugal,[214] which concerned the surveillance of the employee's home for security reasons, the ECtHR found that violation of Article 8 as the legislation, permitting such surveillance, was 'too vague' and 'did not contain any control mechanisms or provide any safeguards for individuals'.[215]

In certain cases, the ECtHR, having established the lack of relevant national legislation, has been satisfied by existing employer's policies which themselves provide some privacy protection to its employees. For example, in cases of obligatory drug tests, such as in Wretlung v. Sweden,[216] the ECtHR noted that the requirement of lawfulness in countries where labour issues were mainly regulated by the parties on the labour market can be satisfied by the establishment of relevant provisions in collective agreements or the employer's policy.[217]

In Köpke v. Germany which concerned covert video surveillance of the cashier, the ECtHR determined the lack of relevant legislation but was satisfied with the developed case law of German courts.[218] These courts elaborated an algorithm for the consideration of similar cases which ensured a careful balancing of the rights of the employees and the employers. Thus, even in the Roman legal system countries where the precedent does not have the role of the source of law, the requirement of

208. A. Joe, 'Workplace Monitoring and the Right to Private Life at Work'. *Modern Law Review* 81:4 (2018): 688-700.
209. ECtHR, Antović and Mirković v. Montenegro (70838/13) 28.11.2017.
210. ECtHR, Malone v. The United Kingdom (8691/79) 02/08/1984, para. 68.
211. *Ibid.*
212. ECtHR, Madsen v. Denmark (58341/00) inadmissible 07/11/2002.
213. ECtHR, M.M. v. UK (24029/07) 13/11/2012, para. 198.
214. ECtHR, Antunes Rocha v. Portugal (64330/01) 31.05.2005.
215. *Ibid.*, paras 74-77.
216. ECtHR, Wretlund v. Sweden (46210/99) inadmissible 09.03.2004.
217. Similar conclusions can be found in ECtHR, Madsen v. Denmark (58341/00) inadmissible 07.11.2002.
218. ECtHR, Köpke v. Germany (420/07) inadmissible 05/10/2010.

'lawfulness' may be satisfied through the establishment of a national judicial approach to cases dealing with the employee's privacy.

The classical illustration of the lawfulness criteria being the key to winning the case on workplace privacy might be found in Antović and Mirković v. Montenegro.[219] It was based on an invasion of privacy complaint brought by two university professors after video surveillance had been installed in areas where they taught. National courts rejected their claims having found that the question of private life had not been at issue as the auditoriums with the cameras were public areas.

The majority of Chamber judges, however, found that Article 8 guarantees a right to 'private life' in the broad sense, including the right to lead a 'private social life' which is the zone of interaction of a person with others, even in a public context.[220] It acknowledged that both covert and non-covert video surveillance of an employee at the workplace is a considerable intrusion into the employee's private life, in particular because the employee, having an obligation to work cannot evade such surveillance.

Having established the interference, the Court went on with the examination of its lawfulness and concluded that the surveillance in question did not comply with the National Personal Data Protection Act, which required consent for the operation of personal data and, therefore, constituted a violation of Article 8.

A very curious example of such an approach to 'lawfulness' may be found in Ribalda and others v. Spain. The Chamber of the ECtHR decided in 2018 that the covert video recording of the supermarket employees constituted a violation because it did not comply with the requirements stipulated in the Spanish Personal Data Protection Act as the employees were not informed about the collection of private data.[221] The Grand Chamber, reconsidering this case, distanced from the analysis of the lawfulness and pointed out that non-compliance with the national law was 'just one of the criteria to be taken into account in order to assess the proportionality of a measure'.[222] The results of further examination of the case demonstrate that the criterion of lawfulness is not decisive at all: the ECtHR found that domestic courts, even though they did not take into account the violation of the relevant national legislation by the employer, fulfilled the State's positive obligations under the ECHR.

The reasoning of the ECtHR in this judgment is rather vague. It acknowledges that the boundaries between the State's positive and negative obligations under the Convention do not lend themselves to precise definitions and that the applicable principles are similar but in the end, it significantly reduces the requirements for compliance with the positive obligations. If the applicable principles were indeed similar, the criteria of lawfulness should have been taken into account by the national courts while assessing the interference with the right to privacy and should have been decisive (as it was in cases Antović and Mirković v. Montenegro[223] or Radu v.

219. ECtHR, Antović and Mirković v. Montenegro (70838/13) 28.11.2017.
220. *Ibid.*, para. 46.
221. ECtHR, López Ribalda and others v. Spain 1874/13 8567/13 (09/01/2018), para. 69.
222. ECtHR, Grand Chamber, López Ribalda and others v. Spain 1874/13 8567/13 (17/10/2019), para. 131.
223. ECtHR, Antović and Mirković v. Montenegro (70838/13) 28.11.2017.

Moldova.[224] Deciding otherwise, in our opinion, might amount to an unfair difference in the treatment of employees who suffered the intrusion with their privacy rights and did not succeed to protect it according to the national law even though such protection should have been granted. We also believe that denying the full underlying value of the lawfulness criteria leaves impermissibly broad the margin of appreciation of the states as far as private employees are concerned.

Having said this, let us proceed with the next criterion which is 'necessity of the interference in the democratic society'.

Is the Interference Necessary in a Democratic Society?

Where the lawfulness of interference has been established, the ECtHR will turn to an analysis of its necessity in a democratic society. This test permits to balance the rights concerned (usually the employee's privacy versus the employer's managerial rights), considering the particular circumstances of the case. For instance, in the case Yilmaz v. Turkey (2019), the claimant was refused an appointment to a teaching post abroad on the grounds of security investigation results concerning his private life (his behaviour at home and his wife's clothing style). Nonetheless, neither the Ministry of Education as an employer nor the local courts provided any grounds or explanations that could justify the refusal to the claimant concerning the public interest or specific public needs and features of educational and teaching services. In this case, the ECtHR found a violation of Article 8 of ECHR explaining that while 'such interference had been in accordance with the law and had pursued one of the legitimate aims referred to in Article 8, [...] in any event it had not been necessary in a democratic society'.[225] Thus, the ECtHR concluded that the use of security investigation results in the claimant's private life was not necessary for making a decision of employing him abroad. Such an interference constituted a violation of the right to respect for private life and was not in compliance with the democratic values of the society despite its legitimate aims (such as public safety).

The two cases (similar to each other) discussed below relate to data protection in the context of the employer's ability to gather urine samples for drug and alcohol tests. The fact scenarios in Madsen v. Denmark[226] and Wretlund v. Sweden are quite similar. In both applications, the employees (Mr Madsen, passenger assistant, and Mr Wretlund, office cleaner at a nuclear plant) argued that the obligatory testing system itself amounted to a violation of their right to private life. Examining the necessity of interference in the democratic society, the ECtHR noted that the need to ensure public safety and the protection of the rights and freedoms of others justified adequate control measures like a random urine test. It is interesting to note that to substantiate this conclusion in Madsen, the Court referred in its deliberations to the Guiding Principles on Drugs and Alcohol Testing Procedures for Worldwide Application in the Maritime Industry adopted by the joint ILO/WHO Committee on the Health of Seafarers in 1993.[227]

224. ECtHR, Radu v. Moldova (50073/07) 15 April 2014.
225. ECtHR, Yilmaz v. Turkey (36607/06) 04.06.2019.
226. ECtHR, Madsen v. Denmark (58341/00) inadmissible 07.11.2002.
227. *Ibid.*

Further, the Court took into account the following circumstances, as established by the national courts:

- employees were appropriately informed about the possibility of such tests being conducted;
- the frequency of tests;
- advance notice;
- coverage of all employees without any exceptions.

An examination of the factors set out above led the ECtHR to conclude that the assumed interferences were, in these instances, justifiable on the basis that they were 'necessary in a democratic society' and declared that each of the applications as being manifestly ill-founded.[228]

The ECtHR's reasoning in these cases matters for Europe because in most European countries, there are no express provisions concerning bodily privacy and approaches differ significantly between jurisdictions.[229]

The ECtHR's approach to the necessity of conducting drug tests on employees might provide general guidelines for finding a balance between the employee's right to privacy and the employer's rights and help members of the CoE create a framework of protection based on the interpretation of the ECHR.

Proportionality of the Interference

Proportionality test is one of the most controversial issues in privacy cases in particular as far as private employees are concerned.[230] In cases concerning the positive obligations of the State under Article 8, the Court verifies if the right to privacy is effectively protected and correctly balanced with the employer's rights by national courts. These are cases of dismissal of employees for non-compliance with their duties revealed by the means of video surveillance (in Köpke v. Germany,[231] Lopez Ribalda and others v. Spain[232]) and by monitoring of private messages sent from corporate Yahoo! messenger account (Bărbulescu v. Romania[233]) and the access of employer to employee's files on the computer (Libert v. France[234]).

It is noteworthy that the two leading cases on employees' privacy were reconsidered by the Grand Chamber of the ECtHR because of the different approaches of the judges to the proportionality of the interference. Thus, in 2016, the Chamber did not find a violation of Article 8 in the case of an engineer, who was dismissed for the use of the company's Internet for personal purposes after his personal messages were read

228. ECtHR, Wretlund v. Sweden (46210/99) inadmissible 09.03.2004, Madsen v. Denmark (58341/00) inadmissible 07.11.2002.
229. A.G. Verstraete & A. Pierce, 'Workplace Drug Testing in Europe', *Forensic Science International* 121:1 (2001): 114.
230. *See* controversial judgments delivered by the Chambers and the Grand Chamber of the ECtHR in cases Bărbulescu v. Romania and López Ribalda v. Spain, and dissenting opinions of judges to each of these four judgments.
231. ECtHR, Köpke v. Germany (420/07) inadmissible 05/10/2010.
232. ECtHR, López Ribalda v. Spain (application No. 1874/13) 09.01.2018.
233. ECtHR, Bărbulescu v. Romania (61496/08) 12/01/2016.
234. ECtHR, Libert v. France (application No. 588/13)22.02.2018.

by the employer (Bărbulescu v. Romania). The ECtHR concluded that the measure was proportionate as the employer did not have another method to verify whether the applicant infringed internal policy. It found that the employer acted within its disciplinary powers and pointed out that the monitoring was limited in scope and proportionate.[235] The Grand Chamber reconsidered the case and delivered the judgment in 2017. By eleven votes to six, it decided that the State has violated its positive obligations under Article 8 and included new factors which should be taken into account by national courts in such cases thus extending the proportionality exercise.[236]

In the case Lopez Ribalda and others v. Spain, the Chamber did not share the domestic courts' view on the proportionality of the measures adopted by the employer because these acts did not comply with the requirements stipulated in the Spanish Personal Data Protection Act. This led the Court to conclude that the domestic courts failed to strike a fair balance between the applicant's right to respect for their private life under Article 8 of the Convention and their employer's interest in the protection of its property rights.[237] It was a good point for excluding covert video surveillance at the workplace as such. Indeed, the employer always has other ways and less intrusive methods to establish the employees' misbehaviour. The Grand Chamber, on the contrary, approved the approach of the national courts in October 2019. It expressed a light criticism of Spanish courts for attaching little attention to the fact of employees' notification about the recording but still concluded that there had been no violation of the ECHR.

These cases represent the lack of a solid approach to the proportionality analysis. It remains too much linked with the perception of the value of privacy by particular judges in particular circumstances, all the judgments referred to above were accompanied by dissenting opinions of judges who balanced the rights of employees and employers in another way.

In 2018, the ECtHR considered the case Libert v. France where an applicant was dismissed after the seizure of his work computer had revealed the storage of pornographic files and forged certificates drawn up for third parties. In contrast with the Bărbulescu case, this application was considered in light of the State's negative and positive obligations under Article 8 as the applicant was employed by a state-owned company. The ECtHR considered that the consultation of the applicant's files pursued a legitimate aim of protecting the rights of employers, who might legitimately ensure that the employees were using the working facilities in line with their obligations and relevant regulations. It considered the French law on workplace privacy protection and established that the existing legislation for the protection of such rights prohibits employers from opening files identified as being '*private*' (*prive*) in the absence of an employee. *Here we have to note that the applicant marked the files in question as 'personal' but not 'private'.* These words can be easily regarded as synonyms. The ECtHR noted that 'admittedly, in using the word 'personal' rather than 'private', the applicant used the same word as that found in the Court of Cassation's case law to the

235. ECtHR, Bărbulescu v. Romania (61496/08) 12/01/2016, para. 60.
236. ECtHR, Bărbulescu v. Romania (61496/08) GC 05/09/2017, para. 121.
237. ECtHR, López Ribalda and Others v. Spain (1874/13 8567/13) 09/01/2018, para. 69.

effect that an employer cannot, in principle, open files identified as 'personal' by the employee'.[238] Despite this finding, the ECtHR proceeded with the conclusion that there had been no violation, having considered the case in its 'entirety' and found the reasoning of the domestic courts sufficient. It also drew attention to the amount of storage space on the employee's work computer to store the files in question (1,562 files representing a volume of 787 megabytes).

We suppose that this reasoning is particularly confusing after the Grand Chamber judgment in Bărbulescu. The point of notification was the most important one in that judgment. It is not clear from first sight why the ECtHR grants less protection to the personal files stored on the employer's computer than to the private messages sent through the employer's account. The ECtHR's reference to the 'entirety' of the case doesn't explain much. In this case, one of the reasons for a narrow approach to workplace privacy protection might be the nature of files discovered by the employer. While the Bărbulescu case was about personal messages with close relatives on sensitive private topics, the Libert case was about porno files and the evidence of fraud committed by the applicant. Supposedly, focusing on whether the words used to denote the files in question could be interpreted as reflecting the private nature of files instead of following common sense in understanding the meaning of the words 'private' or 'personal' allowed the domestic court to find in favour of the employer. The discovery of the gross employee's misconduct during his suspension from work seems to have indirectly served as an additional argument against him in all courts. The ECtHR supported the view of the domestic court, thus signalling that interpretation of the right to respect for private life at work can be narrow and formal if an employee's acts are non-compliant with corporate rules and regulations and commit serious violations (actually, this is the path followed by the Grand Chamber in Lopez Ribalda v. France).

Concluding the paragraph on the Court's framework for the adjudication of cases on workplace privacy, it should be noted that national courts are very attentive to this line of ECtHR's case law. The Bărbulescu case is a champion, being referred to by Constitutional courts,[239] Supreme Courts,[240] Courts of Cassation and first-instance courts.[241] The use of the set of questions elaborated by the ECtHR in the Grand Chamber judgment is particularly important, as it might ensure the harmonious approach to workplace privacy and its balancing with employers' right of control throughout the countries of the Council of Europe.[242] Here, however, the difference in the approach of the Chamber and Grand Chamber to the proportionality of the

238. *Ibid.*, para. 52.
239. Spanish Constitutional Court, judgment of 3 March 2016 (No. 39/2016). *See* López Ribalda and Others v. Spain, para. 56, *see also* Tribunal Constitucional TC (Pleno) Sentencia num. 119/2022 de 20 septiembre RTC\2022\119.
240. *See* Spanish Supreme Court: Tribunal Supremo. Sala de lo Penal, Sentencia núm. 56/2022, 24/01/2022. https://www.poderjudicial.es/.
241. Cour de cassation, civile, Chambre sociale, 25 novembre 2020, 17-19.523; Corte suprema di cassazione, Sez. Lavoro Civile: Sentenza N.34092 Del 12/11/2021; Sentenza N.33380 Del 11/11/2021; Ordinanza N.13266 Del 28/05/2018.
242. In para. 120 the Court formulated the following questions to be answered by national courts in the same cases:

interference and to the factors which have significant value in the consideration of the privacy cases might be a significant obstacle. The Russian Constitutional Court, for example, considering the case about the discloser of confidential information by an employee, referred to the Chamber judgment in the Bărbulescu case stating that 'it is indicative that the ECtHR *found no violation of Article 8* of the ECHR in a case where the employer had accessed employee e-mail messages sent from a work address'.[243] This position was adopted by the Russian court before the Chamber judgment was overruled by the Grand Chamber which came to the opposite conclusion. However, these changes have not been reflected in any further acts of the Russian Constitutional Court, thus neither courts nor other law-enforcement bodies in Russia might not have known about the test elaborated by the Grand Chamber for the cases of workplace privacy violations.

4.2 RIGHT TO WORK, UNFAIR DISMISSAL AND THE VIOLATION OF THE RIGHT TO RESPECT FOR PRIVATE LIFE

In many cases, the ECtHR emphasized that the ECHR does not guarantee either the right to obtain work,[244] general right to employment or the renewal of a fixed-term contract,[245] or a right of access to the civil service or a right to choose a particular profession.[246] However, this omission cannot be interpreted as the ECtHR's reluctance

---

(i) whether the employee has been notified of the possibility that the employer might take measures to monitor correspondence and other communications, and of the implementation of such measures. The notification should normally be clear about the nature of the monitoring and be given in advance;
(ii) the extent of the monitoring by the employer and the degree of intrusion into the employee's privacy (a distinction should be made between monitoring of the flow of communications and of their content, whether all communications or only part of them have been monitored, was monitoring limited in time and the number of people who had access to the results, were their spatial limits to the monitoring);
(iii) whether the employer has provided legitimate reasons to justify monitoring the communications and accessing their actual content (monitoring of the content of communications requires weightier justification);
(iv) whether it would have been possible to establish a monitoring system based on less intrusive methods and measures than directly accessing the content of the employee's communications;
(v) the consequences of the monitoring for the employee subjected to it and the use made by the employer of the results of the monitoring operation;
(vi) whether the employee had been provided with adequate safeguards, especially when the employer's monitoring operations were of an intrusive nature;
(vii) i)whether an employee whose communications have been monitored have access to a remedy before a judicial body with jurisdiction to determine, at least in substance, how the criteria outlined above were observed and whether the impugned measures were lawful. ECtHR, Bărbulescu v. Romania (61496/08)GC 05/09/2017, para. 120.

243. Judgment of the Constitutional Court of the Russian Federation of 26 October 2017. N 25-P.
244. ECtHR, Panfile v. Romania (13902/11) 20/03/2012, para. 18, Sobczyk v. Poland (25693/94 and 27387/9510 February 2000; Dragan Cakalic v. Croatia (17400/02)15 September 2003; Torri and Others v. Italy and Bucciarelli v. Italy (11838/07 and 12302/07) 24/01/2012.
245. ECtHR, Fernández Martínez v. Spain (56030/07) GC 12/06/2014, para. 109.
246. ECtHR, Denisov v. Ukraine (76639/11) GC 25/09/2018, para. 100.

to acknowledge the basic or fundamental character of the right to work. The right to work could be incorporated into Article 8 by interpreting it as saying that work is an inherent part of private life. As Sen said: 'Employment can be an element of self-respect, and also of the other people's respect towards a person.'[247]

We have already cited above the Court's approach to work as to a 'significant, if not the greatest, opportunity of developing relationships with the outside world' expressed in the Niemitz case in 1992.[248] This reading is very consonant to the interpretation of the right to work by the UN Committee on Economic, Social and Cultural rights (CESCR). In its General Comment No. 18, the Committee stated: 'the right to work is essential for realizing other human rights and forms an inseparable and inherent part of human dignity ... the respect for the individual and his dignity is expressed through the freedom of the individual regarding the choice to work, while emphasizing the importance of work for personal development ...'.[249] Also, it is worth noting that the ECtHR in several cases referred to the norms of the ESC on the right to work.[250]

The ECtHR in the recent twenty years became less categorical about the absence of the right to obtain work and acknowledged the rights of applicants which were closely linked with this right. For example, in Campagnano v. Italy,[251] the ECtHR found a violation of Article 8 as the applicant was unable to engage in any professional or business activity on account of the entry of her name in the bankruptcy register. In Mateescu v. Romania,[252] it found a violation of Article 8 as the applicant was not allowed to simultaneously practice two professions in the private sphere. The conclusion of the Court in Demirel v. Turkey, discussed in Chapter 3, might be added to this line of cases; however, the part of the judgment where the refusal to hire the applicant was found to be in violation of the ECHR remained without reasoning.[253] Also in the recent case,[254] the Court found that the refusal to appoint a person for the job position might be considered a violation of Article 8 if the grounds of such refusal evidence the interference with the applicant's private life. This conclusion can also be interpreted as the Court's indirect support of the right to work. The recent development of the ECtHR's legal reasoning in the cases on unfair dismissal made scholars presume the

247. A. Sen Emploi, 'Institutions et technologie: Quelques problèmes de politique générale', *Revue international de travail*. 135:3-4 (1996): 488.
248. ECtHR, Niemietz v. Germany (13710/88) 16/12/1992, par. 29.
249. UN CESCR, *General Comment No. 18: The Right to Work (Article 6 of the Covenant)*, 6 February 2006, E/C.12/GC/18, available at, https://www.refworld.org/docid/4415453b4.html (accessed 15 September 2022).
250. *See* at least: Sidabras and Džiautas v. Lithuania (55480/00, 59330/00) 27/07/2004, Campagnano v. Italy (7955/01) 23/03/2006.
251. ECtHR, Campagnano v. Italy (77955/01) 23/03/2006.
252. ECtHR, Mateescu v. Romania (No. 1944/10) 14/01/2014.
253. *See* comments of A. Timmer, Of Firearms and Weak Women: Sex Discrimination in Hülya Ebru Demirel v. Turkey, 31.07.2018, https://strasbourgobservers.com/2018/07/31/of-firearms-and-weak-women-sex-discrimination-in-hulya-ebru-demirel-v-turkey/#more-4206 (accessed 20 December 2022).
254. ECtHR, Yılmaz v. Turkey (application No. 36607/06) 04.06.2019.

emergence of 'a human right to protection against unjustified dismissal'.[255] The right to be protected against unlawful dismissal is recognized to be a part of the right to work by the CESCR in General Comment No. 18.[256]

Turning to the consideration of cases about dismissal under Article 8 we should first refer to the judgment in Denisov v. Ukraine,[257] where the ECtHR explained in detail the relevance of Article 8 to the dismissal cases and established certain criteria for the evaluation of the level of severity of the alleged violation of Article 8 (*see* paragraphs 100-114 in Annex 1).

The Grand Chamber pointed two ways in which a private life issue would usually arise in such a dispute concerning dismissal: either because of the underlying reasons for the dismissal (it was called the 'reason-based approach') or because of the consequences of it for the applicant's private life ('consequence-based approach').[258] The reason-based approach takes place 'when the impugned measure was based on reasons encroaching upon the individual's freedom of choice in the sphere of private life' (paragraph 103). It might be illustrated by the Bărbulescu[259] or Lopez Ribalda cases discussed above in paragraph 4.1. In these cases, the employees were dismissed because the employer gathered information about their misconduct through covert video surveillance or secret monitoring of the messages thus interfering with their right to respect for private life.

The reason-based approach might be taken by the Court if the impugned measure (the dismissal) has or may have serious negative effects on the individual's private life. In particular, the ECtHR divides the possible negative consequences into three groups: (i) impact on the individual's 'inner circle', in particular where there are serious material consequences; (ii) the individual's opportunities 'to establish and develop relationships with others'; and (iii) the impact on the individual's reputation (paragraph 107). It also states that 'convincing evidence showing that the threshold of severity was attained' is an intrinsic feature of the consequence-based approach within Article 8. The applicants are obliged to identify and explain the concrete repercussions on their private life and the nature and extent of their suffering, and to substantiate such allegations in a proper way. Speaking separately about the impact of dismissal on the reputation, the Court held that an attack on a person's reputation must attain a certain level of seriousness and be made in a manner causing prejudice to personal enjoyment of the right to respect for private life; this requirement covers social reputation in general as well as professional reputation in particular (paragraph 112).

It should be noted that in none of the cases on unfair dismissals, the Court clearly distinguished the difference between the first and the second group of circumstances. Never in its case law, the violation was found only being based on 'serious material consequences'. As it was correctly pointed out by the British Court of Appeal, the matters listed by the ECtHR are to a greater or lesser extent involved in every

255. H. Collins, 'An Emerging Human Right to Protection Against Unjustified Dismissal', *Industrial Law Journal* 50:1 (2021): 36-69, https://doi.org/10.1093/indlaw/dwaa003.
256. CESCR, General Comment No. 18, adopted on 24 November 2005. E/C.12/GC/186, para. 35.
257. ECtHR, Denisov v. Ukraine (76639/11) GC, 25 September 2018, paras 100-117.
258. *Ibid.*
259. ECtHR, Bărbulescu v. Romania (61496/08) 12/01/2016.

dismissal.[260] Therefore, the main attention should be focused on the evaluation of the severity of the impact of the dismissal upon those aspects of private life and which might be only established on a case-by-case basis. Further, we will consider the examples of reason-based and consequences-based approaches to the cases of unfair dismissal.

The former was applied in Mile Novaković v. Croatia, considered in 2020.[261] The applicant complained about dismissal in 1999 for giving his classes in Serbian rather than in Croatian. Being a Serb, he had lived and worked in Croatia for most of his professional life in the area which had been peacefully reintegrated into Croatian territory after the war. The authorities alleged that his dismissal was lawful as he could not teach in Croatian and thus did not correspond to the requirements set for teachers. They also substantiated that the measure was proportionate as he could not be expected to learn Croatian because of his old age at that time (he was 55). The case was brought under Articles 8 and 14, and Article 1 of Protocol No. 12 (general prohibition of discrimination) but was considered only under Article 8. The ECtHR assumed that both the language and the age of a person, which were underpinning reasons for the dismissal, constitute essential aspects of an individual's private life (paragraph 48). Thus, the Court established that there had been an interference with his right to respect for his private life. Considering the justifications for the interference, the Court stated that it was 'in accordance with the law', but the factor of the necessity of the interference was not met. The inspection, which triggered the applicant's dismissal was performed only concerning four teachers of Serbian ethnic origin, following an anonymous complaint by pupils of Croatian origin. The dismissal was the strictest available measure and the State did not provide significant reasons for the non-provision of the employee with additional training (paragraphs 57-70). This reasoning made the Court conclude that the applicant's dismissal from work was not proportionate to the aim sought to be achieved and violated Article 8 of the Convention.

We suppose that, in this case, the Court might have justified the application of Article 8 both by reason-based and consequence-based approaches. The latter might be substantiated through the reference to the right to establish relationships with others, including relationships of a professional nature.[262] In any case, in our opinion, this judgment is evidence of the openness of the ECtHR to the consideration of the cases relating to unfair dismissal under Article 8.

The consequence-based approach even if not named as such was first established in Volkov v. Ukraine, the case on dismissal of the Supreme court's judge. In that case, the Court stated the following:

> the dismissal of the applicant from the post of judge affected a wide range of his relationships with other persons, including relationships of a professional nature. Likewise, it had an impact on his 'inner circle' as the loss of his job must have had tangible consequences for the material well-being of the applicant and his family.

260. Vining v. London Borough of Wandsworth [2017] EWCA Civ 1092.
261. ECtHR, Mile Novaković v. Croatia (73544/14)17.12.2020.
262. ECtHR, C. v. Belgium (21794/93) 07/08/1996, para. 25.

> Moreover, the reason for the applicant's dismissal, namely breach of the judicial oath, suggests that his professional reputation was affected.[263]

We see that in this stance, the Court referred to all three groups of circumstances, without considering any of them separately.

The same reasoning might be found in the case brought by eighteen Ukrainian judges dismissed from their positions as a result of disciplinary proceedings.[264] In each case, the High Council of Justice of Ukraine found that the applicants had breached the judicial oath; these rulings were submitted to Parliament or to the President of Ukraine for final decisions on their dismissal. Final decisions were later unsuccessfully challenged before the courts. The applicants complained that their dismissal proceedings violated the principle of an independent and impartial tribunal and also that their private lives had been substantially affected by their dismissals. Thus, they claimed the violation of Articles 6 and 8 of the Convention.

The Court's judgment, in this case, is very brief and refers to its findings in Oleksandr Volkov,[265] concluding that the proceedings against the applicants were not in compliance with the principles of independence and impartiality. In the same way, the Court estimated the applicants' arguments on the violation of Article 8 – just repeating the conclusions in the Volkov case. However, in the Volkov case, the Court required the State to reinstate the applicant, which was an exceptional and even unique measure in the case law of the ECtHR. In Kulykov and Others v. Ukraine, the Court refused the claims for reinstatement, stating in particular:

> The Court notes that at the present time a full-fledged judicial reform is taking place in Ukraine which includes constitutional and further legislative amendments, as well as institutional changes ... given the scope and the circumstances of the present applications, it cannot be concluded that this substantially new background renders the relevant domestic procedures prima facie futile and useless.[266]

This stance demonstrates again that the Court's ruling to reinstate the unlawfully dismissed judge is an 'exotic' remedy provided only in exceptional cases against particular countries where domestic civil procedures have been found in general ineffective.

In Denisov v. Ukraine (2018),[267] the ECtHR also applied the consequence-based approach. Mr Denisov was dismissed from his role as president of the Kyiv Administrative Court of Appeal for managerial inefficiency but continued to serve as a regular judge for the same Court. The ECtHR established that the grounds for the dismissal had nothing to do with his private life, and the dismissal itself did not affect it. In particular,

263. ECtHR, Volkov v. Ukraine, para. 166.
264. Kulykov and Others v. Ukraine (5114/09, 4588/11, 9740/11, 12812/11, 20554/11, 35336/11, 68443/11, 75790/11, 78241/11, 5678/12, 11775/12, 21546/12, 54135/12, 65207/12, 77810/12, 242/13, 15073/13, and 57154/13) 19/01/2017.
265. In particular to the fact that the procedure before the HCJ and Parliament had disclosed a number of structural and general shortcomings which had compromised the principles of independence and impartiality. *Ibid.*, paras 101-109.
266. *Ibid.*, para. 148.
267. Denisov v. Ukraine (application No. 76639/11) GC 25.09.2018.

it found that the lower salary, the reduction of his prospective pension benefits and the loss of the prestigious position in the circumstances of the cases did not amount to severe impact of the dismissal upon his 'inner circle' (paragraph 122). Also, the applicant continued to work as an ordinary judge and he remained at the same court alongside his colleagues. Thus, his right to establish and maintain relationships was not significantly affected. Finally, with regard to the reputation of the applicant, the ECtHR stated that the case involved only his managerial skills, while his professional role as a judge was not touched upon. This limited area of scrutiny and criticism cannot be regarded as relating to the core of the applicant's professional reputation (paragraph 126). Therefore, his dismissal could hardly be regarded as a violation of Article 8 of the ECHR. This allowed the ECtHR to declare the complaint inadmissible under Article 8.

In 2019, the ECtHR considered the case of five Ukrainian civil servants who were dismissed as the result of lustration process.[268] This case is important for at least two reasons: it sets out the grounds for non-compliance of the Ukrainian law on lustration with the ECHR and provides a new example of finding that the dismissal is a violation of the right to respect for private life based on a consequence-based approach.

Let us consider these points consequently. In a number of cases, the Court has found that lustration measures engaged the applicants' right to respect for their private life, as they affected their reputation and/or professional prospects.[269] The Government Cleansing (Lustration) Act, enacted was adopted in 2014 to ensure the loyalty of civil servants and dismiss those who had either held their position for at least one year during the Yanukovych regime (2010-2014), held certain positions within the Communist Party prior to 1991, or who had failed to file lustration declarations. This law also provided a maximum ten-year ban for civil service. This is the first case when the Court had to deal with the 'new lustration' cases *not connected with the work of the totalitarian State. Even though the ECtHR in principle admitted the possibility of such law to decrease the politicisation of the civil service,*[270] *the severity of the chosen measures had the contrary effect. It was underlined that these measures were constructed as a sort of collective liability for working under Mr Yanukovych, with no estimation of any individual role of the applicants in any antidemocratic developments. The Court noted the lack of proportionality of the impugned measures, in particular the fact that the decisions about dismissals had been made publicly available even before any review of those decisions by courts, the ban for service imposed for ten years, the lack of attention to the individual situations of the applicants.*[271]

Considering the dismissal of the applicants as a violation of the right to respect for private life, the Court noted that they were not merely suspended, demoted or transferred to positions of lesser responsibility, but dismissed and excluded from the

268. POLYAKH AND OTHERS v. UKRAINE (58812/15 53217/16 59099/16) 17/10/2019.
269. ECtHR, Sõro v. Estonia (22588/08), 3/09/2015, Karajanov v. the former Yugoslav Republic of Macedonia (2229/15) 6/04/2017, Naidin v. Romania, No. 38162/07, 21/10/2014, ECtHR, Sidabras and Dziautas v. Lithuania (55480/00 59330/00) 27/07/2004.
270. Paragraph 278.
271. One of the applicants was dismissed solely on the grounds of providing his lustration report five days later.

civil service altogether, losing all their remuneration with immediate effect.[272] Taking into account the imposed ban on civil service and the publication of the relevant information in open-access sites, the Court held that there had been a violation of Article 8 in respect of all five applicants. Interestingly, in another case on lustration and the dismissal from the post of the Supreme Court judge,[273] the ECtHR did not refer to the Denisov case or to a consequence-based approach for the consideration of such cases. Mr Samsin failed to submit a lustration declaration needed under the law and was banned from employment in the civil service until the end of 2024. His name was put in a publicly accessible Lustration Register. He tried to resign but his resignation application was not considered. He was deprived of the benefits associated with judicial retirement despite being close to retirement age. The Court found that these measures had not been necessary for a democratic society and constituted an interference with the right to respect for private life. It noted that the legitimate aim might have been achieved if the applicant's resignation was accepted and found a violation of Article 8. It was only briefly noted in the part of the admissibility analysis that the applicant suffered considerable prejudice in terms of retirement payments to which he was entitled (paragraph 42). Also, it was stated that the consideration expressed in Volkov v. Ukraine about the consequences of a dismissal for material well-being and reputation were equally applicable in the present case (paragraph 41). No illustration of the Court's severe approach to the evidence of the impact of the dismissal on three aspects of private life might be found here, thus questioning the consistency of the Court's analysis of similar cases.

Concluding the paragraph on unfair dismissals, some words should be said about the special group of cases – the dismissals of judges. This group is constantly rising. In 2021, there were seven cases (one of them united the applications of eight judges) considered under Articles 6, 8 and 10 of the Convention. The applicants claimed that their dismissals, transfer to lower positions or suspension form work violated the ECHR. Interestingly, two of these seven cases are about the violations in respect of the leaders of the professional judges' unions: Miroslava Todorova,[274] the President of the Bulgarian Union of Judges, and Mr Eminağaoğlu,[275] the Chairman of Yarsav, an association of judges and prosecutors. Further, we will first review the cases considered under Articles 6 and 8 of the ECHR, the latter two cases of the union leaders will be analysed in the part dedicated to freedom of expression.

Under Article 6 of the ECHR, everyone is entitled to a fair and public hearing within a reasonable time by an independent and impartial tribunal established by law *in the determination of his civil rights and obligations* or of any criminal charge against him. Provided the special character of public service as a whole and of the work of judges in particular, the Court had to elaborate the special conditions permitting to establish whether the claim of a public servant concerning the conditions of work might be considered as relating to a 'civil right'. The case law concerning the

272. Paragraph 209.
273. ECtHR, Samsin v. Ukraine (38977/19) 14.10.2021.
274. ECtHR, Miroslava Todorova v. Bulgaria (40072/13) 19/10/2021.
275. ECtHR, Eminağaoğlu v. Turkey (76521/12) 09.03.2021.

applicability of Article 6 to disciplinary proceedings against civil servants refers to the 'Vilho Eskelinen test':[276] the State cannot rely on an applicant's status as a civil servant to exclude him or her from the protection afforded by Article 6 unless two conditions are fulfilled.[277] First, domestic law must have expressly excluded access to a court for the post or category of staff in question – or implicitly, as later clarified in Grzęda v. Poland.[278] Second, the exclusion must be justified on 'objective grounds in the State's interest'.[279]

The test was applied in the recent cases brought by applicants who were dismissed, transferred or suspended or prevented from exercising the functions of a judge.[280] In none of the seven cases, the Court found that the exclusion of access to a court was justified on objective grounds in the State's interest. In Bilgen v. Turkey,[281] the Court considered the case about the transfer of a senior judge at the Ankara Regional Administrative Court without his consent to another court in a lower judicial district by a decree of the High Council of Judges and Prosecutors that had not been subject to judicial review. Applying the Eskelinen test, the Court determined that while the first condition was met, the second one was not satisfied. Considering the case under Article 6, it underlined that there should have been procedural safeguards to ensure that judges' judicial autonomy was not jeopardized by undue external or internal influences and that only very weighty reasons might justify the absence of judicial review. It stated that denying the applicant access to a court for an important career matter had not pursued a legitimate aim and could have potentially damaged judicial independence and had thus violated his rights, finding a violation of Article 6.

In Gumenyuk and Others v. Ukraine, the former Supreme Court of Ukraine judges claimed that unlawful prevention from exercising judicial functions after legislative reform and the inability to contest it violated Articles 6 and 8 of the ECHR. The legislative reform was later declared unconstitutional. The ECtHR stated that it must be particularly attentive to the protection of members of the judiciary against measures affecting their status or career that can threaten their judicial independence and autonomy (paragraph 71). The necessity to have in place procedural safeguards and the possibility of appeal against decisions affecting the career, including the status, of a judge is widely acknowledged because what is at stake is public trust in the functioning of the judiciary. Restriction of the right of a member of the judiciary to contest their premature dismissal or a measure which amounts to constructive

276. ECtHR, Eskelinen and Others v. Finland (63235/00) 19 April 2007, para. 94.
277. Guide on Article 6 of the ECHR Right to a fair trial (civil limb) Updated to 30 April 2022. https://www.echr.coe.int/documents/guide_art_6_eng.pdf.
278. ECtHR, Grzęda v. Poland [GC] (43572/18) 15/03/2022, cited from ECtHR Guide on Article 6.
279. Guide on Article 6 of the ECHR Right to a fair trial (civil limb) Updated to 30 April 2022. https://www.echr.coe.int/documents/guide_art_6_eng.pdf.
280. For example, ECtHR, Gumenyuk and Others v. Ukraine (11423/19) 22.7.2021; Eminağaoğlu v. Turkey (76521/12)09.03.2021, Xhoxhaj v. Albania (15227/19) 09/02/2021, Loquifer v. Belgium (79089/13, 13085/14 and 54534/14) 20.07.2021 (the ECtHR found the violation of Article 6 because of the absence of a judicial remedy to review the suspension by the High Council of Justice of one of its members who is not a magistrate and to obtain the annulment or suspension of the execution of this decision).
281. ECtHR, Bilgen v. Turkey (1571/07) 09.03.2021.

dismissal may be incompatible with the independence of the judiciary, where such measure is without any specific reason (paragraph 72). It concluded that the applicants should have, in principle, enjoyed direct access to the court in respect of their allegations of unlawful prevention from exercising their judicial functions and found a violation of Article 6. It also found a violation of Article 8 as, due to the legislative amendments, they were 'deprived of the opportunity to continue judicial work and to live in the professional environment where they could pursue their goals of professional and personal development'. This case, along with Baka v. Hungary, are remarkable examples of the possibility to protect the rights of judges and their independence when the changes in their status/mandate were brought by law.

The research of the ECtHR's jurisprudence under Article 8 demonstrates that the Court significantly contributed to establishing the standards of employees' privacy protection, providing the framework for the consideration of such cases (*see* Bărbulescu v. Romania), acknowledging a link between private life and employment, stating that unfair dismissal might violate the right to respect for private life and elaborating three groups of consequences which might evidence the violation (*see* Denisov v. Ukraine). This approach, as noticed by scholars, 'can shield an individual employee against employer domination', a possibility that was absent in countries such as the United Kingdom before its incorporation of the ECHR.[282]

Summing up the approach of the ECtHR to dismissal formed in and after the Denisov v. Ukraine case, the following might be outlined:

- the chances for bringing the case on unfair dismissal are particularly rising for those applicants who were dismissed from public service or by the state;
- there have been no cases yet where the consequences-based approach was applied in case of the horizontal application of the Convention, which is not excluded though;
- the three groups of circumstances which are distinguished by the ECtHR and assessed in the cases of consequence-based dismissal should also form a part of proportionality analysis in unfair dismissal cases by national courts;
- the applicant in such cases should be able to demonstrate the severe impact of dismissal upon (i) the individual's 'inner circle', (ii) opportunities 'to establish and develop relationships with others', and (iii) the individual's reputation.

282. V. Mantouvalou, 'Human Rights and Unfair Dismissal: Private Acts in Public Spaces'. *Modern Law Review* 71:6 (2008): 939.

CHAPTER 5
Employee's Freedom of Thought, Conscience, Religion and Expression

In this chapter, we will consider how the case law of the ECtHR protects the human rights of employees at the workplace or in connection to work.

5.1 FREEDOM OF THOUGHT, CONSCIENCE AND RELIGION

Article 9

1. Everyone has the right to freedom of thought, conscience and religion; this right includes freedom to change his religion or belief and freedom, either alone or in community with others and in public or private, to manifest his religion or belief, in worship, teaching, practice and observance.
2. Freedom to manifest one's religion or beliefs shall be subject only to such limitations as are prescribed by law and are necessary in a democratic society in the interests of public safety, for the protection of public order, health or morals, or for the protection of the rights and freedoms of others.

There are several areas when freedom of religion or belief interacts with the field of labour law (perceived broadly): the right to contentious objection to military service;[283] workers' rights to manifest religion or belief at work;[284] religious organizations' rights to impose religious requirements on their staff.[285]

In the last five years, the ECtHR considered several cases on the right to contentious objection to military service, while there were no judgments on the two remaining areas. This is why we will first consider the new cases and then proceed with a brief explanation of the Court's approach to the right to manifest religion or belief at work and say a few words about the difference of the approach to this right of the

283. ECtHR, Bayatyan v. Armenia (23459/03) 27 October 2009.
284. ECtHR, Eweida and others v. The United Kingdom (48420/10) 15 January 2013.
285. ECtHR, Siebenhaar v. Germany (18136/02) 3 February 2011; *See* L. Vickers, 'Freedom of Religion or Belief and Employment Law'. *Religion & Human Rights* 12:2-3 (2017): 165.

ECtHR and the Court of Justice of the European Union (CJEU) in light of Achbita case, considered by the CJEU in 2017. The religious organizations' rights to impose religious requirements on their staff will not be considered in the absence of the new case law; the information might be found in the first book,[286] where the relevant cases were considered in detail.

5.1.1 The Right to Contentious Objection to Military Service

In Baratyan v. Armenia, the ECtHR acknowledged the right of conscientious objection to military service, absent from the text of Article 9, thus establishing a common standard for the countries of the CoE.[287] The Grand Chamber stated that although Article 9 does not explicitly refer to a right to conscientious objection, the opposition to military service, where it is motivated by a serious and insurmountable conflict between the obligation to serve in the army and a person's conscience or his deeply and genuinely held religious or other beliefs, constitutes a conviction or belief of sufficient cogency, seriousness, cohesion and importance to attract the guarantees of Article 9.[288] The Court had an opportunity to develop its view on how should the alternative service be organized in order to comply with Article 9 of the ECHR in 2017.

The applicants in Adyan and Others v. Armenia[289] were Jehovah's witnesses; they were convicted of evading conscription to military and alternative service and sentenced to two and a half years' imprisonment. They had argued in their defence that the alternative service provided for under domestic law was not of a genuinely civilian nature, as it was supervised by the military authorities, and was punitive in nature as it lasted forty-two months compared to twenty-four months for military service.

The Court stated that the fact of provision of the right to alternative service to conscientious objectors 'is not sufficient to conclude that the authorities have discharged their obligations under Article 9 of the Convention'.[290] It further formulated the two key requirements for the organization of the alternative service: it should be of a genuinely civilian nature and not deterrent or punitive in character.

Considering the nature of the work which the applicants had to perform, ECtHR stated that the kind of the work performed is 'only one of the factors to be taken into account when deciding whether alternative service is of a genuinely civilian nature'. Such factors as authority, control, applicable rules and appearances, and uniformity may also be important for the determination of that question (paragraphs 68-69). Having established that the military authorities were actively involved in the supervision of that service, the judges concluded that the alternative labour service was not

286. E. Sychenko, 'Individual Labour Rights as Human Rights: The Contributions of the European Court of Human Rights to Worker's Rights Protection'. Roger Blanpain, Frank Hendrickx (eds). *Wolters Kluwer International. Bulletin of Comparative Labour Relations*, Vol. 96 (2017), Chapter 6.
287. ECtHR, Bayatyan v. Armenia (23459/03) 27 October 2009.
288. *Ibid.*, para. 110.
289. ECtHR, Adyan and Others v. Armenia (75604/11) 12/10/2017.
290. *Ibid.*, para. 69.

sufficiently separated hierarchically and institutionally from the military system and, therefore, the alternative service was not of a genuinely civilian nature.

Analysing the character of the alternative service, the Court underlined the importance of the duration factor and referred to the opinion of the European Committee of Social Rights (ECSR) expressed in respect of Greece (paragraph 48). In its Conclusions XIX-1 of 24 October 2008, the ECSR stated that under Article 1 § 2 of the ESC, alternative service may not exceed one and a half times the length of armed military service. In the present case, the duration of the alternative service was almost two times more than military service; the ECtHR held that such difference in the duration 'can be said to have contained a punitive element'. On the basis of those two factors, the Court concluded that 'the authorities failed, at the material time, to make appropriate allowances for the exigencies of the applicants' conscience and beliefs and to guarantee a system of alternative service that struck a fair balance between the interests of society as a whole and those of the applicants, as required by Article 9 of the Convention'.

It is interesting to note that this judgment was referred to by some scholars from countries which are not part of the Council of Europe as marking the significant development of the human rights requirements for the organization of alternative service.[291] Also, this case might be named a landmark one as it is establishing the criteria for the evaluation of the alternative service organization in light of Article 9 of the ECHR. It is a valuable tool for those countries which have not yet introduced such an opportunity in their legislation. In the CoE, there is no law on conscientious objection in Turkey and Azerbaijan;[292] in Ukraine, there was an expansion of the mandatory military service and enforcement of conscription without exceptions for conscientious objectors in 2021.[293] Thus, this judgment also provides legal reasoning for possible national attempts to protect the rights of such people in these countries and grounds for the application before the ECtHR.

5.1.2 Workers' Rights to Manifest Religion or Belief at Work

The approach of Strasbourg bodies to protect the manifestation of one's religion or belief in the workplace has significantly changed over the years. The former European Commission of Human Rights was reluctant to acknowledge the link between an employee's refusal to fulfil employment obligations and the right to manifest his or her religious beliefs.[294]

---

291. *See* Korean researcher: 심민석. (2019). 대체복무제도의 제한조건과 양심적 병역거부 – 유럽인권재판소의 판례를 중심으로 – 유럽헌법연구, (31), 243-280. (M. Shim, 'Restrictions on Alternative Service and Conscientious Objection: Focusing on the Jurisprudence of the European Court of Human Rights'. *European Constitutional Studies* 31 (2019): 243-280).

292. *See* A. Yiannaros, 'The Criminalisation of Conscientious Objection to Military Service in Turkey and Azerbaijan: Time for Action?'. *International Journal of Human Rights and Constitutional Studies* 8:3 (2021): 197-217.

293. European Bureau for Conscientious Objection. Annual Report Conscientious Objection to Military Service in Europe 2021, https://www.ohchr.org/sites/default/files/2022-05/EBCO-HRC50.pdf.

294. EurCommHR, Konttinen v. Finland (24949/94) inadmissible 3 December 1996; Stedman v. UK (29107/95) inadmissible 9 April 1997.

Recent case law demonstrates that, in contrast with the approach of the Commission, the ECtHR is developing the 'better approach' by properly considering the proportionality of interference. It stated, for example, that certain restrictions on the freedom to manifest one's religion or belief might be justified by the requirements of a particular job, particularly when public servants or judges are concerned. The Convention does not rule out the imposition of a duty of discretion or restraint on civil servants with a view to safeguarding the neutrality of the public service and ensuring respect for the principle of secularism.[295] In Pitkevich v. Russia,[296] the ECtHR emphasized that the States have a wide margin of appreciation in determining whether the interference with a judge's freedom to manifest his religion was proportionate to the aim of maintaining the authority and impartiality of the judiciary.

In Sodan v. Turkey,[297] the Court had to consider in light of Articles 9 and 8 the applicant's transfer from a senior post within the governor's office in the capital to a similar post in the provinces following a report on his conduct pointing out that his wife wore an Islamic veil. It noted that some restrictions on the rights of public servants under Article 9 might be justified by the requirement of the State's neutrality, but the applicant was impartial in the performance of his duties and was not engaged in religious fundamentalism. It stated that the mere proximity or membership, real or supposed, of the applicant to a religious movement cannot constitute sufficient reason in itself to take an unfavourable measure against him (paragraph 54).

Finally, in the case of Eweida v. UK about the positive obligations of the state under Article 9, *the Court* stated: 'Given the importance in a democratic society of freedom of religion, the ECtHR considers that, where an individual complains of a restriction on freedom of religion in the workplace, rather than holding that the possibility of changing job would negate any interference with the right, the better approach would be to weigh that possibility in the overall balance when considering whether or not the restriction was proportionate.'[298] Thus, the ECtHR has abandoned the Commission's view that the freedom to manifest one's belief might be protected by resigning from the post and has started to balance the freedom of the employee to manifest his or her religion in the workplace as against the rights of his or her employer, referring to the possibility to resign as only one additional factor in the overall balance. This approach permitted the Court to find the violation of Article 9 in the case of Ms Eweida, who was suspended from work for wearing a cross as, in the opinion of the national courts, it might have had a negative impact on British Airways' brand or image, which attempted to underline their neutrality. ECtHR held that prohibiting Ms Eweida from wearing her cross was not of crucial importance to the employer as the cross was a discrete one and the uniform code of the company was further changed, allowing her to wear visible religious symbolic jewellery.[299] Therefore, balancing the

295. ECtHR, Guide on Article 9 of the ECHR. Updated on 31 August 2022, https://www.echr.coe.int/documents/guide_art_9_eng.pdf.
296. ECtHR, Pitkevich v. Russia (47936/99) inadmissible 8 February 2001.
297. ECtHR, Sodan v. Turkey (18650/05) 02/02/2016.
298. ECtHR, Eweida and other v. UK (48420/10) 15 January 2013, para. 83.
299. *Ibid.*, para. 95.

applicant's right with the right of the employer to establish a uniform code, the ECtHR gave priority to the rights of Ms Eweida.

This case attached a lot of attention from human rights and labour law scholars particularly not only in the UK but also in other European countries.[300] It was welcomed as establishing 'a factual scenario where the rights of the religious employee in a secular work environment trump the desires of her employer'.[301] Another wave of the popularity of this case started in 2017 when the Court of Justice of the EU considered the famous Achbita case[302] about the dismissal of a woman for refusing to stop wearing an Islamic headscarf at the workplace. In this case, the CJEU found that 'an employer's wish to display an image of neutrality towards customers relates to the freedom to conduct a business, as recognised in Article 16 of the Charter, and is, in principle, legitimate, in particular where the employer involves only those employees who are supposed to come into contact with the employer's customers in pursuing that objective'.[303] This stance was criticized as 'affirming an employer's right to indulge the prejudices of its customers'.[304] Scholars confronted the approaches of the two European courts to the issue of employers' regulations prohibiting workers from wearing visible religious signs at work. Almost unanimously[305] they argued that the CJEU conclusion in Achbita was in contrast with the approach of the ECtHR and that the former afforded too much weight to the interests of the employer.[306]

The CJEU indeed opted to protect the interest of the employer in these particular circumstances, however, it should be held in mind that the balancing exercise depends largely on a particular set of circumstances, both on the part of an employee and an employer. In the Achbita case, the employer was, in contrast with British Airways

300. M. Pearson, 'Article 9 at a crossroads: interference before and after Eweida'. *Human Rights Law Review* 13:3 (2013): 580-602; H. Hill, '"Eweida v. United Kingdom": The Right to Manifest Religion under Article 9 of the ECHR'. *European Human Rights Law Review* 2 (2013): 187-193; B. van der Stegen, La liberté religieuse dans la vie professionnelle: du neuf depuis l'arrêt Eweida et autres c. Royaume-Uni?. Faculté de droit et de criminologie, Université catholique de Louvain, 2016. Prom.: Dorssemont, Filip, http://hdl.handle.net/2078.1/thesis:7280; E. Carmona Bayona, 'Libertad religiosa y relaciones laborales. Estudios de las sentencias más emblemáticas del Tribunal Europeo de Derechos Humanos y del Tribunal Constitucional Español'. *Derecho global. Estudios sobre derecho y justicia* 6:16 (2020): 239-250; C. Maioni, 'I simboli religiosi nella giurisprudenza europea tra libertà religiosa e libertà di impresa (Religious Symbols in European Case Law: Limits to Religious Freedom in Workplace)'. *University of Milano-Bicocca School of Law Research Paper* 18:08 (2018).
301. J. Maher, 'Eweida and Others: A New Era for Article 9?'. *International & Comparative Law Quarterly* 63:1 (2014): 213-233.
302. CJEU, Grand Chamber, Samira Achbita and Centrum voor gelijkheid van kansen en voor racismebestrijding v G4S Secure Solutions NV, 14 March 2017, No. C-157/15.
303. *Ibid.*, para. 38.
304. A. Hambler, 'Neutrality and Workplace Restrictions on Headscarves and Religious Dress: Lessons from *Achbita* and *Bougnaoui*', *Industrial Law Journal* 47:1 (2018): 149-164, https://doi.org/10.1093/indlaw/dwx033.
305. With the exception of Morwarid Hashemi, '2019/29: Eweida versus Achbita: A Storm in a Teacup (EU), 2019'. Eur. Emp. L. Cases 174 (2019).
306. For example, Vickers, 'Achbita and Bougnaoui: One Step Forward and Two Steps Back for Religious Diversity in the Workplace', *European Labour Law Journal* 8: 3 (2017): 232-257; S. Riggins, 'Limitations of the Right to Manifest Religion in European Private Companies: Achbita v. G4S Secure Solutions NV under Article 9 of the ECHR and Article 18 of the ICCPR', *American University International Law Review* 33:4 (2018): 977-1018.

in Eweida, consequent and systematic in implementing his neutrality policy (paragraph 40), even if it was not written at the beginning of her employment. Also, the CJEU numerously underlined that the interference was held proportionate because she had direct contact with the employer's customers. This is why it was held necessary to achieve the aim of displaying, in relations with both public and private sector customers, a policy of political, philosophical or religious neutrality.

Also, it should be mentioned that CJEU refers[307] to the Eweida case in its legal reasoning and, in particular to the paragraph about the proportionality of the interference. Thus, it acknowledges the relevance of other instruments and other bodies in the human rights field[308] and also seems to share the importance of the proportionality exercise in consideration of cases on the freedom of religion at work.

Concluding the paragraph on the freedom of religion and worker's rights there is a need to formulate the achievements of the Court in the recent five years. The judgment in respect of Ms Eweida remains the biggest contribution of the ECtHR to the evaluation of proportionality of the interference with the employee's right to manifest one's religion at the workplace when the employer imposes the regulations prohibiting the exposure of any religious symbols. However, in contrast with the Bărbulescu case, which is cited by national courts when similar cases are considered, we haven't found any reference to this judgment in Italian, French or Spanish cases relevant to employment law[309] and few references in the UK. In particular, British courts relied on paragraph 82 of the Eweida judgment, where the Court explained what does the manifestation of one's religion mean. This test was used by British courts in cases on a dismissal of a practising Christian, who held the position of Non-Executive Director of an NHS Trust, for commenting in media that it is 'not normal' for a child to be adopted by a single-parent or a same-sex couple.[310] Also, it was applied in a case evaluating the recruitment policy which stipulated that only heterosexual evangelical Christians could be accepted as potential carers.[311] In both cases, the Courts did not find a violation of Article 9 of the ECHR.

The most important contribution of the Court in recent years has been, in our opinion, in elaborating quality requirements to the regulation of alternative service for the contentious objectors to military service. Having established already in 2009 in Baratyan v. Armenia, the right of conscientious objection to military service, the Court,

307. CJEU, Achbita case, para. 39.
308. The idea is borrowed from A.C.L. Davies, 'One Step Forward, Two Steps Back? The Viking and Laval Cases in the ECJ'. *Industrial Law Journal* 37:2 (2008) 126-148, https://doi.org/10.1093/indlaw/dwn001.
309. We have checked the following databases, https://www.poderjudicial.es/search/indexAN.jsp (for Spanish judgments), https://www.legifrance.gouv.fr/ and https://www.courdecassation.fr/acces-rapide-judilibre (for French), https://justice.ge.ch/fr/contenu/jurisprudence (Geneva), https://lesentenze.it/cercasentenze (Italian case law).
310. Page v. NHS Trust Development Authority [2019] UKEAT 0183_18_1906 (19 June 2019) URL, http://www.bailii.org/uk/cases/UKEAT/2019/0183_18_1906.html; Page v. NHS Trust Development Authority [2021] EWCA Civ 255 (26 February 2021) URL, http://www.bailii.org/ew/cases/EWCA/Civ/2021/255.html).
311. Cornerstone (North East) Adoption and Fostering Services Ltd, R. (On The Application Of) v. HM Chief Inspector of Education, Children's Services and Skills (OFSTED) [2021] EWCA Civ 1390 (24 September 2021) URL, http://www.bailii.org/ew/cases/EWCA/Civ/2021/1390.html.

eight years later, formulated in Adyan and Others v. Armenia, the two key requirements for the organization of the alternative service. In the opinion of the ECtHR, it should be of a genuinely civilian nature and not deterrent or punitive in character. It also listed the factors which are relevant for the establishment of the nature and character of the alternative service: the kind of work performed, authority, control, applicable rules and appearances, uniformity, and the importance of the duration factor. Hopefully, these judgments will pave the way for changes in a number of countries of the Council of Europe, where the norms on alternative service are still absent or do not correspond to the standards developed by the ECtHR.

5.2 EMPLOYEE'S FREEDOM OF EXPRESSION

Article 10 of the ECHR has much in common with Articles 9 and 8 but provides more grounds for the justification of interference. Under Article 10, everyone has the right to freedom of expression. This right shall include freedom to hold opinions and to receive and impart information and ideas without interference by public authority and regardless of frontiers. Under paragraph 2 of this article, the exercise of these freedoms, since it carries with it duties and responsibilities, may be subject to such formalities, conditions, restrictions or penalties as are prescribed by law and are necessary in a democratic society, in the interests of national security, territorial integrity or public safety, for the prevention of disorder or crime, for the protection of health or morals, for the protection of the reputation or rights of others, for preventing the disclosure of information received in confidence, or for maintaining the authority and impartiality of the judiciary.

The ECtHR stated the exceptions provided in paragraph 2 must be narrowly interpreted and the necessity for any exceptions must be convincingly established.[312] The scope of employees' freedom of expression differs from the general scope of the citizen's freedom of expression as employment relations impose the duty of loyalty which also means certain restraint of this freedom. The number of cases of employees' freedom of expression is growing as due to digital technologies and the development of social networks, it has become very easy for an employer to access the opinion of an employee exposed on a Facebook page or even in the form of a 'like' to a certain post and then prove it in court.

The majority of the Strasbourg jurisprudence on the violation of Article 10 in the context of employment relations concerns the rights of public servants. The ECtHR has reiterated repeatedly that employees owe their employer a duty of loyalty, reserve and discretion.[313] The research of relevant case law does not allow us to define these notions separately and clearly. In the majority of cases, these duties are listed in order to remind us of the special character of employment relations in general and of public servants in particular, attaching particular weight to the special fiduciary character of

312. ECtHR, Steel and Morris v. The United Kingdom (68416/01) 15 February 2005, para. 87.
313. *See* ECtHR, Langner v. Germany (14464/11) 17 September 2015, para. 43; Vogt v. Germany (17851/91) 26 September 1995, para. 53; Matuz v. Hungary (73571/10) 21 October 2014, para. 32; Pay v. The United Kingdom (32792/05) inadmissible 16 September 2008.

employment relations especially as far as public servants being representatives of the State are concerned.

However, the ECtHR has pointed out that the requirement to act in good faith in the context of an employment contract does not imply an absolute duty of loyalty towards the employer or a duty of discretion to the point of subjecting the worker to the employer's interests.[314] The scope of these obligations depends on the particular position of the employee, on the public interest in the disclosed information (in case of disclosure) and even on the historical background of a particular country.[315]

Considering the exceptions listed in paragraph 2 of Article 10, the balancing of the freedom of expression of the employee, bound by the duty of loyalty, against the right of employers to manage their staff or the right to reputation becomes a key to finding a violation. Here, the difference between public and private employees, the roles of the employees in their employment and in building the reputation of the employer are important. For example, the right of public servants to publicly criticize their employer, the State, is granted in exceptional situations when the ECtHR considers that the information made public has indisputable social value and must be known to the citizens.[316] As far as private employees are concerned, their duty of loyalty, reserve and discretion 'could not be as strong as the duty of loyalty and reserve required of members of the civil service'.[317] Also, the ECtHR has pointed out that the requirement to act in good faith in the context of an employment contract does not imply an absolute duty of loyalty towards the employer or a duty of discretion to the point of subjecting the worker to the employer's interests.[318]

Further, we will consider the application of these principles in the cases considered by the ECtHR in the recent five years.

In 2017, it considered one case on the employee's freedom of expression, balancing this right with the employer's right to protect the reputation. In Marunić v. Croatia,[319] the applicant complained that her dismissal from the post of the director of a municipal utility company on account of statements she had made to the media was in breach of Article 10 of the ECHR. In the publication in question, she alleged that the problems with the company's performance, which she headed, had been caused by the municipality, which required the utility company to act unlawfully. Later on, she was dismissed on the grounds that her public statements had been damaging to the company's reputation.

Considering this claim, the Court attached attention to the fact that the applicant's publication was a reply to the publication criticizing her work made by the mayor of the Kostrena Municipality eight days before. It was noted that 'the right of

314. ECtHR, Palomo Sánchez and others v. Spain [GC] (28955/06 et al.) 12 September 2011, para. 76.
315. *See* ECtHR, Vogt v. Germany, also Joint Dissenting Opinion of Judges Bonello, Strážnická, Bîrsan, Jungwiert and Del Tufo in Maestri v. Italy (39748/98) GC 17 February 2004.
316. ECtHR, Panioglu v. Romania (33794/14) 8.12.2020; Kudeshkina v. Russia (29492/05) 26 February 2009.
317. ECtHR, Melike v. Turkey (35786/19) 15/06/2021, para. 48.
318. ECtHR, Palomo Sánchez and others v. Spain [GC] (28955/06 et al) 12/09/2011, para. 76.
319. ECtHR, Marunić v. Croatia (51706/11) 28.03.2017.

rectification or of reply, as an important element of freedom of expression, falls within the scope of Article 10 of the Convention'.[320]

The applicant's choice of ways to reply did not violate her duty of loyalty as according to the ECtHR's case law, the right to reply may be exercised on the same forum where the criticism was published.[321] Researching the question of whether the applicant exceeded the limits of permissible criticism, the Court found that her allegation of unlawful activities of the company she headed should be considered not as a statement of fact but rather as a value judgment.[322] For these reasons, it was concluded that the applicant's statements did not exceed the limits of permissible criticism and therefore her dismissal was not 'necessary in a democratic society' for the protection of the business reputation and the rights of the company she headed.

In our opinion, this judgment broadens the scope of the freedom of expression of public employees as it acknowledges the right to defend themselves through the use of the same forum, where criticism was made public, thus overweighting the duty of loyalty and discretion and leaving as unnecessary the question of whether there were any other available effective means of remedying the wrongdoing which the applicant intended to uncover.[323]

In 2019, the Court considered a case[324] on a private employee's freedom of expression. The case concerned the applicant's dismissal from his job in human resources (HR) at a bank after publishing articles on the website devoted to HR issues. Those articles, in the opinion of the employer, had breached its confidentiality standards and infringed on financial interests. The applicant argued that the articles related to changes in personal income tax regulations and did not have any direct connection with his employer. National courts (including the Constitutional court) refused to consider the case in light of the employee's freedom of expression, supposing that articles on professional topics could not benefit from free speech protection as were not of a general public interest.

The ECtHR did not agree with this approach, stating that 'workplace-related free speech does not only protect comments that demonstrably contribute to a debate on a public matter!'[325] Further, it noted that neither the employer nor the *national courts* made any attempt to demonstrate in what way the speech in question could have adversely affected the business interests. The Court concluded that the domestic authorities had failed to demonstrate convincingly that the rejection of Mr Herbai's challenge to his dismissal had been based on a fair balancing of each party's rights and violated Article 10 of the ECHR.

One of the commentators noted that this judgment leaves a question as to what degree employers may limit employees' free speech when these employees are

320. *Ibid.*, para. 50.
321. *Ibid.*, para. 54.
322. *Ibid.*, para. 61.
323. ECtHR, Guja v. Moldova [GC] (14277/04) 12/02/2008, 73.
324. ECtHR, Herbai v. Hungary (11608/15) 05/11/2019.
325. *Ibid.*, para. 42.

discussing topics (on open-access platforms) within their area of work expertise.[326] We suppose that free speech about professional matters might be limited only to the extent which is proved to be necessary for the protection of the reputation or other interests or rights of an employer, so it largely depends on the particular circumstances of the case.

A number of recently considered cases concerned the freedom of expression of judges and prosecutors. The case Kövesi v. Romania,[327] the chief prosecutor of the National Anti-Corruption Directorate (DNA) of Romania, should be considered in more detail. Ms Kövesi is a remarkable figure in Romania. The major progress on the anti-corruption front in the country was largely associated with her nomination in 2013; during her tenure, the DNA's national and international profile rose dramatically as Western media, such as The Guardian (Gillet 2015) and The New York Times (Higgins 2014), sang her praises.[328] In February 2018, the Minister of Justice proposed that the applicant be removed from office, referring, among other things, to three Constitutional Court decisions adopted in connection with the activity of the DNA and to public statements she had made. The President of Romania refused to sign the dismissal decree, which prompted a complaint to the Constitutional Court by the Prime Minister. In May 2018, the Constitutional Court ordered the President to sign the decree, finding, among other things, that neither the President nor the Constitutional Court was authorized to assess the reasons put forward by the Minister of Justice in his proposal.[329] The applicant complained that her mandate as chief prosecutor of the DNA had been terminated as a result of the views concerning legislative reforms affecting the judiciary that she had expressed publicly, in her professional capacity. The ECtHR, after ascertaining the violation of Article 6 paragraph 1,[330] and that there was an incontrovertible causal link between the exercise of the applicant's freedom of expression and the termination of her mandate, also ascertained that the measure of early removal of the applicant was not 'necessary in a democratic state', entailing an undue encroachment of the executive into the judiciary and threatening the independence of the latter.[331] In fact, Ms Kovesi, in her capacity as the DNA chief prosecutor – whose duties also included opinions on legislative reforms that could have had an impact on

326. D. Mangan, 'Does an Online Professional Profile Violate an Employer's Confidentiality?'. *European Labour Law Journal* 12:1 (2021): 102-104.
327. ECHR, Kövesi v. Romania, No. 3594/19, 5.05.2020.
328. E. Chrun, 'Help Me Help You: How the EU Made Romania's Anticorruption Reforms a (Temporary) Success'. *East European Politics* (2022): 1-21.
329. ECtHR. Romania violated the rights of anti-corruption directorate chief prosecutor when dismissing her before the end of her mandate. Press release. ECHR 123 (2020) 5 May 2020.
330. The removal from the position of chief prosecutor of the DNA had, in fact, been assumed by the President on a proposal from the Minister of Justice with the endorsement of the CSM, without any judicial review of the legitimacy of the decision, exposing the appellant to the mercy of a complete discretion of the executive power. More precisely, any possibility of judicial review had been limited to the formal nature of the removal decree, but any type of examination of the reasons that had led to the decision had been prevented internally. As a result, the internal judicial remedies available to the appellant could not be said to be sufficient and the right to a fair trial had been violated. ECHR, Kövesi v. Romania, No. 3594/19, 5.05.2020.
331. The Court recalled the previous case Wille v. Liechtenstein (Wille v. Liechtenstein, No. 28396/95, 28.10.1999) in which the president of the administrative court had received a letter of reprimand from the Prince of Liechtenstein due to the statements expressed in a public

the independence of the judiciary – and in a debate of extreme public interest, had expressed statements of a purely professional nature which required a high degree of protection of his freedom of expression and strict control over any kind of external interference. The Court found that 'the premature termination of the applicant's mandate was a particularly severe sanction, which undoubtedly had a "chilling effect" in that it must have discouraged not only her but also other prosecutors and judges in future from participating in public debate on legislative reforms affecting the judiciary and more generally on issues concerning the independence of the judiciary' (paragraph 209).

This judgment was met with much enthusiasm by scholars. It was named as 'historical' and as 'undoubtedly likely to strengthen the independence of the judiciary, the independence of the prosecutors, but also to encourage the participation of judges and prosecutors in debates on the independence and modernization of the justice system in Romania'.[332] This case continues the long line of ECtHR's cases on the independence of the judiciary and the prosecutors, supporting the struggle of those public servants who try to voice out the shortcomings of the system and challenge the way of things.[333]

In Goryaynova v. Ukraine,[334] the ECtHR considered the application of the former prosecutor at the Odessa regional prosecutor's office, who was dismissed after publishing an open letter on the internet to the Prosecutor General of Ukraine in which she highlighted systematic corruption and illegal activities within his Office. It should be noted that before that, she sent some reports to the Prosecutor General of Odessa to make him aware of such conduct, but he had not taken them into account and had even pressured her to resign from her office; several letters sent to the Prosecutor General of Ukraine remained without reply. Considering the case, the Court reminded that signalling by a public sector of illegal conduct in the workplace should, in certain circumstances, enjoy protection. The ECtHR stated that in certain situations, it is necessary to prioritize the public's significant interest in specific information, even if it means overriding a legal obligation of loyalty. This is particularly crucial when the employee is the only individual with knowledge of the wrongdoing, making them the most suitable person to act in the public's best interest by informing the general public (paragraph 50). Considering this case, the Court found that the national courts did not investigate the key factors to be established in such cases: the veracity of the statements, the motivations, the possibility of actually raising them to the superiors, the existence of damage to the public prosecutor following the statements or the opportunity for less serious sanction than dismissal. Thus, given the lack of pertinent and sufficient reasons to justify the dismissal, the interference with the applicant's

conference by the magistrate, in which he had found a violation of Article 10. In fact, in the letter, the prince announced that he wanted to sanction him because of his opinions on some constitutional law issues.

332. D. Calin, The Recent ECtHR Judgment Kövesi v. Romania: Reactions of Romanian Authorities and Implications Regarding the Rule of Law (8 January 2022). Strasbourg Observers, 16 June 2020, available at SSRN, https://ssrn.com/abstract=4003862.
333. *See also* Baka v. Hungary, Kudeshkina v. Russia.
334. ECHR, Goryaynova v. Ukraine, No. 41752/09, 8.10.2020.

freedom of expression was found disproportionate and violated Article 10 of the Convention.

This judgment was called by scholars as 'recognising a genuine right of critical denunciation-alert'.[335] In our opinion, such a right already was part of the Court's general approach to the freedom of expression of judges and other public officials of a high rank. Particularly, this point was developed in the first case of Kudeshkina v. Russia,[336] where the Court found a violation of Article 10 even if she 'allowed herself a certain degree of exaggeration and generalisation'.[337]

In 2021, there were at least three important cases on the freedom of expression of employees. The first one is Melike v. Turkey case.[338] It concerned the dismissal of Ms Melike, a contractual cleaner at the Ministry of National Education, for having clicked 'Like' on various Facebook articles (posted on the social networking site by a third party). The posts which she 'liked' were about the Kurdish people being massacred (*received six 'likes' in total*), criticism of the ruling political party (*14 'likes' in total*), an insult to the leader of a publicly known religious group (*no information about the total number of 'likes'*). These 'likes' were considered a severe violation and constituted the offences 'committing acts and deeds containing physical violence, sexual harassment and threats of any kind' and of 'disturbing the peace, tranquillity and order of the workplace for ideological and political purposes, boycotting or occupying, engaging in conduct aimed at preventing the conduct of public services and provoking and encouraging such acts' (paragraph 7). National courts supported the dismissal. The ECtHR noted several very important points which, in our opinion, should constitute a framework for the consideration of similar cases by national courts:

(1) The duty of loyalty, confidentiality, and discretion that employees owe to their employers may not be as stringent as the duty of loyalty and discretion expected from civil service members.
(2) The act of adding a 'Like' to content could not be considered to carry the same weight as sharing content on social networks, in that a 'Like' merely expressed sympathy for the content published, and not an active desire to disseminate it.
(3) Given the nature of her position, Ms Melike could have had only limited renown and representative status in her workplace and her activities on Facebook could not have had a significant impact.
(4) The national authorities had not specified in their decisions if the 'likes' were noticed or complained of by pupils, parents, teachers or other employees in

335. M.M. Yanini, 'Libertad de crítica de la persona trabajadora como derecho de alerta: de la lucha contra la corrupción a la protección medioambiental: Comentario a la Sentencia del Tribunal Europeo de Derechos Humanos de 8 de octubre de 2020 (Goryaynova vs. Ukraine)'. *Revista de Trabajo y Seguridad Social CEF* (2020): 207-215.
336. The case was about the dismissal of a judge for public accusations against the President of the Moscow City Court, which were made during the applicant's election company for the post of the deputy of the State Duma. ECtHR, Kudeshkina v. Russia (29492/05) 26 February 2009.
337. ECtHR, Kudeshkina v. Russia, para. 95.
338. ECtHR, Melike v. Turkey (35786/19) 15.06.2021.

her workplace and whether those 'likes' had given rise to incidents of such a nature as to jeopardize order and peace in the workplace.

(5) The authorities had not sought to assess the potential of the 'Like' comments in question to cause an adverse reaction in the applicant's workplace, having regard to the content of the material to which they related, the professional and social context in which they were made and their potential scope and impact.

The Court concluded that there was no reasonable relationship of proportionality between the interference with Ms Melike's right to freedom of expression and the legitimate aim pursued by the national authorities and found the violation of Article 10.

The second case under Article 10 was considered against Turkey. In Eminağaoğlu v. Turkey,[339] the Court considered disciplinary sanctions of the judicial officer for his statements and criticisms, particularly about high-profile cases in the media. The Court found the shortcoming of the decision-making process and the violations of Article 6. It noted that the disciplinary process was not surrounded by the guarantees that were indispensable for the applicant's status as a judicial officer and chairman of an association of judges and prosecutors. The ECtHR concluded that the restrictions imposed on the applicant's freedom of expression had not been accompanied by effective and adequate safeguards against abuse and therefore violated Article 10.

The third case, Miroslava Todorova v. Bulgaria,[340] was about the dismissal of a judge and President of the Bulgarian Union of Judges who criticized the Supreme Judicial Council (SJC) concerning certain appointments of court presidents, as well as the government's policy on the judiciary, especially with regard to the defence of judicial independence. The investigation revealed serious breaches of her professional duty: she had the largest number of delayed cases, fifty-seven in total, and the reasons were issued with delays of up to over three years (paragraph 19). She had been subject to an initial sanction of a two-year reduction in salary and had then been dismissed, and this penalty had been replaced by a two-year demotion. In the opinion of the ECtHR, the 'chain of events tended to indicate that the main reason for these audits had been a wish to penalise the applicant, rather than a legitimate wish to correct excessive delays in judicial proceedings'. It further established that the main aim of the sanctions had not been to ensure compliance with the time limits for concluding cases but to penalize and intimidate her on account of her criticism of the SJC and the executive. The dismissal was found to have a chilling effect on the applicant and also on other judges, deterring them from voicing critical opinions on the action of the SJC, or more generally on issues relating to judicial independence. In the conclusions, the Court on the one side establishes that the domestic authorities had failed to explain why the sanctions imposed on the applicant had been necessary and proportionate to the legitimate aims pursued in the present case. On the other, it states that the finding, in this case, did not rule out the possibility of prosecuting judges for breaches of their professional duty following the exercise of their freedom of expression, provided that

339. ECtHR, Eminağaoğlu v. Turkey (76521/12) 09.03.2021.
340. ECtHR, Miroslava Todorova v. Bulgaria (40072/13) 19/10/2021.

such action could not be suspected of constituting retaliation for the exercise of that fundamental right. This reasoning was called 'confused' by a commentator.[341] It somehow reminded the balancing of the duty of loyalty of the judges against the freedom of expression in Kudeshkina v. Russia. In that case, the ECtHR pointed out that the freedom of expression targeted at criticizing the judiciary should be more restricted taking into account the importance of judges to enjoy public confidence to fulfil their duties.[342] The arguments of the ECtHR in Todorova v. Bulgaria are a message to the national bodies competent to consider disciplinary cases on judges' misconduct, to keep track of the need to ensure the independence of the judiciary and the freedom of expression of judges.

Concluding the paragraph on the freedom of expression in the context of employment relations (and relations of public service) the following points of the Court's recent case law are worth emphasizing:

- the Court acknowledged the right of rectification or of reply, as an important element of freedom of expression (*see* Marunić v. Croatia);
- it recognized that workplace-related free speech does not only protect comments that demonstrably contribute to a debate on a public matter but covers also topics of purely professional interest if it does not adversely affect the business interests of an employer (*see* Herbai v. Hungary);
- it provides a set of questions to be answered by national courts in the cases on the expression of an opinion in the social network through 'likes' (*see* Melike v. Turkey);
- and last, but definitely not least, it continues to support the independence of judges in the countries of the CoE, urges the States to take into account the 'chilling effect' which disciplinary measures imposed for the expression of a certain opinion might have on public servants, and ensure the proportionality of the interference with the legitimate aim pursued (*see* Goryaynova v. Ukraine, Todorova v. Bulgaria, Kövesi v. Romania).

341. T. Mortier, M. Todorova V. Bulgaria: Bulgaria Joins List of Serious Rule of Law Offenders, 8 December 2021, https://strasbourgobservers.com/2021/12/08/miroslava-todorova-v-bulgaria-bulgaria-joins-list-of-serious-rule-of-law-offenders/.
342. ECtHR, Kudeshkina v. Russia (29492/05) 26/02/2009.

Chapter 6

The Evolution of the Court's Approach to Collective Labour Rights

Article 11 of the ECHR, under the heading 'Freedom of Assembly and Association', grants explicitly to every person the right to participate in the formation of trade unions and to join them for the specific purpose of defending one's interests. This is both a right - where the term 'right' underlines the positive aspect of pretension - and a freedom - which indicates the negative aspect of non-compulsion. The second paragraph of the article in question then provides that the exercise of these rights may not '*be subject to restrictions other than those which are established by law and which constitute measures necessary, in a democratic society, for national security, public safety, the defense of order and the prevention of crime, the protection of health or morals, and the protection of the rights and liberties of others. This article does not preclude legitimate restrictions from being imposed on the exercise of these rights by members of the armed forces, the police, or the state administration*'.

This second paragraph thus recognizes a discretion for national legislative systems in applying the Convention's institutions and guarantee tools to concrete cases, making use of the canon of 'democratic society' as the valve criterion for national legislation to restrict the freedom recognized by the Convention. Democratic society is connoted by pluralism, tolerance and a spirit of openness, and demands a balance that ensures that minorities are treated fairly and that any abuse of dominance is avoided.[343] It is noteworthy that both the ECHR and the UN Convention on Economic, Social and Cultural Rights give the notion of a 'democratic society' a particularly prominent role in the position of limits to the protections offered by the Conventions with respect to the legislative policy choices of Member States: indeed, in many articles of the Conventions, measures established by national law can integrate as many limits to the application of the conventional norm, indeed, for many articles of

343. For an in depth analysis on how human rights can be used to shape the future of labour law, *see* P.M. Collins, *Putting Human Rights to Work: Labour Law, the ECHR, and the Employment Relation*, Oxford University Press. Oxford 2022.

the Conventions, measures established by national law can integrate as many limits to the application of the conventional norm as needed, provided that the measures and the limits are respondents to the canon of necessity of a democratic society.

Trade union freedom, as recognized by Article 11, has nonetheless been interpreted extensively over time by the European Court of Human Rights, on the one hand valorizing negative trade union freedom, and on the other, recognizing the right to strike as an inseparable corollary of the right of trade union association. The reference is to the famous cases Demir and Baykara v. Turkey[344] ('Demir'), on collective bargaining, and Enerji Yapi-Yol Sen v. Turkey[345] ('Enerji'), on strike action, in which the Court recognized 'indirect' protection for the right to strike through the guarantee of one of the few 'social rights' expressly enunciated in the Convention: the right to form and join trade unions for the protection of one's interests (Article 11). The Court on that occasion for the first time recognized '*the organic link between freedom of association and freedom to bargain collectively*' and consequently, the possibility of invoking Article 11 of the ECHR as a protective umbrella for collective action rights.

Prior to the fundamental turning point brought about by the Demir case, and following on with the 2009 Enerji ruling, the Strasbourg Court used to affirm that it was not possible to extrapolate specific modalities of trade union action from Article 11 to deem them to be included in the generic protection of the right to form and join trade unions, it being sufficient that the state system guarantees the right of trade unions to 'make their voices heard'.[346]

The ECHR was evidently once seen as a tool for securing only civil and political rights, nothing more. This was the standard because the Council of Europe was really cautious in drawing a line between what was safeguarded under the sanction of the European Court of Human Rights and what was not - the socioeconomic rights included in the ESC. Hence, the ECHR did not and does not specifically identify the right to engage in collective bargaining, much alone the right to strike, as a direct consequence of what is stipulated in Article 11.

It follows that early decisions of the ECtHR reveal that the original scope of Article 11 was significantly narrower than it is now. To show how things have changed, it will be useful to (briefly) touch three specific cases: National Union of Belgian Police v. Belgium[347] ('Belgian Police'), Swedish Engine Drivers' Union v. Sweden[348] and Schmidt and Dahlström v. Sweden.[349]

In the Belgian Police case, the Court held that the words 'for the protection of his interests' in Article 11(1) 'show that the Convention safeguards freedom to protect the occupational interests of trade union members by trade union action, the conduct and development of which the Contracting States must both permit and make possible. In

344. Case of Demir and Baykara v. Turkey No. 34503/97 (ECtHR, 12 November 2008).
345. Case of Enerji Yapi-Yol Sen v. Turkey No. 68959/01 (ECtHR, 21 April 2009).
346. Starting with the case of Schmidt and Dahlström v. Sweden No. 5589/72 (ECtHR, 6 February 1976). *See* A. Guazzarotti, 'Articolo 11', in: S. Bartole, P. De Sena, V. Zagrebelsky, *Commentario breve alla CEDU, Cedam*, 2012, 447.
347. Case of National Union of Belgian Police v. Belgium No. 4464/70 (ECtHR, 27 October 1975).
348. Case of Swedish Engine Drivers' Union v. Sweden No. 5614/72 (ECtHR, 6 February 1976).
349. Case of Schmidt and Dahlström v. Sweden, cited (4).

the opinion of the Court, it follows that the members of a trade union have a right, in order to protect their interests, that *the trade union should be heard*'.

It holds however a very important distinction: this 'right to be heard' doesn't have to be manifested or allowed in any specific way since, the Court follows: '*the Article does not guarantee any particular treatment of trade unions, or their members, by the State, such as the right to be consulted by it*'.[350] Therefore, it is left to each individual State to choose the means by which to safeguard this newfound right, be it by consultation or by various other kinds of activity vis-à-vis the Government, for instance, to present claims and to make representations for the protection of the interests of its members or certain of them, as long as the steps taken are not ignored by the Government itself.

In the Swedish Engine Drivers' Union case, the exact same logic was applied, supporting the conclusion that the right to *collective bargaining is 'not an element necessarily inherent in a right guaranteed by the Convention*' but '*the members of a trade union have a right, in order to protect their interests, that the trade union should be heard*'.[351]

Lastly, in the Schmidt and Dahlström case, it was held – citing the Belgian Police case – that: 'The Court recalls that the Convention safeguards freedom to protect the occupational interests of trade union members by trade union action, the conduct and development of which the Contracting States must both permit and make possible [...]. Article 11 para. 1 (art. 11-1) nevertheless leaves each State a free choice of the means to be used towards this end. *The grant of a right to strike* represents without any doubt one of the most important of these means, but there are others. Such a right, which *is not expressly enshrined in Article 11* (art. 11), may be subject under national law to regulation of a kind that limits its exercise in certain instances.'

According to this early legal interpretation, Article 11 only allowed a limited and general right to freedom of association, which excluded more specific rights to certain activities. It did not safeguard any specific tools for securing this freedom, such as the ability to strike or engage in collective bargaining. But, it is only in the context provided by these early cases that the extreme relevance of some of the Court's more recent case law can be really understood.

A fundamental median step in the growth of the embrace of meanings of Article 11 as intended by the Court was the recognition that it protects also a negative right – the right not to join an association.

350. The Court also stated: '*trade union matters are dealt with in detail in another convention, also drawn up within the framework of the Council of Europe, namely the Social Charter of 18 October 1961. Article 6 para. 1 of the Charter binds the Contracting States "to promote joint consultation between workers and employers". The prudence of the terms used shows that the Charter does not provide for a real right to consultation. Besides, Article 20 permits a ratifying State not to accept the undertaking in Article 6 para. 1. Thus it cannot be supposed that such a right derives by implication from Article 11 para. 1 (art. 11-1) of the 1950 Convention, which incidentally would amount to admitting that the 1961 Charter took a retrograde step in this domain*'. This, as it will be shown further, is just one of the times in which the Court cited the ESC's clauses as justification for not protecting these more specific rights.

351. Again, the Court uses the ESC as a mean of interpretation of the ECHR lesser role in granting or recognizing this kind of rights, reporting *verbatim* what it held in the *Belgian Police* case.

The first time this issue was raised was in the case of Young, James and Webster v. the United Kingdom,[352] where the British Government contended that this negative right had been deliberately excluded from the Convention and that this was demonstrated by the following passage in the travaux préparatoires:

> On account of the difficulties raised by the 'closed-shop system' in certain countries, the Conference in this connection considered that it was undesirable to introduce into the Convention a rule under which 'no one may be compelled to belong to an association' which features in [Article 20 para. 2 of] the United Nations Universal Declaration.[353]

On that occasion, the Court did not consider it necessary to explicitly answer the question.

The subsequent case in the matter was Sigurdur A. Sigurjonsson v. Iceland,[354] where, against the opinion of the travaux préparatoires, this 'negative' aspect of the right was recognized in a peculiar passage: the Court held that '*the Convention is a living instrument which must be interpreted in the light of present-day conditions*' and therefore Article 11 '*must be viewed as encompassing a negative right of association. It is not necessary for the Court to determine in this instance whether this right is to be considered on an equal footing with the positive right*'. On the same line were Sørensen and Rasmussen v. Denmark[355] ('Sørensen') and Vörđur Ólafsson v. Iceland[356] in the following years.

In more recent years then, with reference to the Demir case, the Court declared Turkey's violation of Article 11 ECHR, in that the national authorities had adopted conduct that deterred and hindered the exercise of trade union freedom, which is recognized by international sources and national practice indifferently to public and private employees. The Court, on the one hand, identifies the right to collective bargaining as an essential element of the right to constitute and join a trade union, protected by Article 11 ECHR; on the other hand, it sees no valid grounds for prejudicing the exercise of the collective right, given that public employees, except for certain particular areas (police force, army, etc.),[357] must be treated in the same way as private employees and, above all, there are no public interests that justify any limitation of trade union freedom.[358]

352. Case of Young, James and Webster v. The United Kingdom Nos 7601/76 and 7806/77 (ECtHR, 13 August 1981).
353. Report of 19 June 1950 of the Conference of Senior Officials in Collected edition of the 'Travaux préparatoires' of the European Convention on Human Rights/Council of Europe – The Hague: Martinus Nijhoff, 1977, Vol. IV, p. 262.
354. Case of Sigurdur A. Sigurjónsson v. Iceland No. 16130/90 (ECtHR, 30 June 1993).
355. Case of Sørensen and Rasmussen v. Denmark Nos 52562/99 and 52620/99 (ECtHR, 11 January 2006).
356. Case of Vörđur Ólafsson v. Iceland No. 20161/06 (ECtHR, 27 April 2010).
357. *See* below, Chapter 3 of the present part of the volume.
358. The Court stated that: '*having regard to the developments in labour law, both international and national, and to the practice of Contracting States in such matters, the right to bargain collectively with the employer has, in principle, become one of the essential elements of the "right to form and to join trade unions for the protection of* [one's] *interests" set forth in Article 11 of the Convention, it being understood that States remain free to organise their system so as, if appropriate, to grant special status to representative trade unions*'.

This open approach was apparently short-lived, since the following cases did not carry it forward but, instead, scaled back, relegating it as a borderline case.[359] For the purpose of this analysis, it suffices to say that the road to the recognition of the right to collective bargaining has been arduous and is still to come to an end. The meaning and the impact of the latest decisions of the Court on this right will be analysed in the following chapter.

Similarly, in the Enerji case, the Court found a violation of Article 11 ECHR by Turkey in the face of a regulatory act inhibiting the union from organizing a strike aimed at the recognition of the right to collective bargaining. The measure was deemed unlawful in that it introduced a restriction on the exercise of trade union freedom that, in addition to being unjustified, appeared disproportionate to the ends pursued.

These apparently worker-friendly departures from the Court's previous jurisprudence in the decisions in Belgian Police and Schmidt were as unpredicted as surprising, being defined as '*epoch-making ruling*'[360] and as a '*judicial revolution*'.[361,362]

In actuality, the Court didn't really distance itself from the Schmidt and Dahlström case, where the right to strike was described as one of the many, albeit one of the most important, means to protect occupational interests. The Court just stated that there needs to be a 'pressing social need' to interfere with the right to strike, one of the rights enshrined in Article 11 of the Convention.

Henceforth, the debate over the precise extent of the protection of the right to strike has blossomed, since the Court has further recognized that the right to strike is protected by Article 11, but it has left open the question of whether the right is an essential element of freedom of association or not.

There are a series of successful applications alleging a violation of the right to strike, especially against Turkey;[363] however, other decisions raise uncertainty over how far the Court is willing to extend its protection.[364]

359. In particular, *see* case National Union of Rail, Maritime and Transport Workers v. The United Kingdom No. 31045/10 (ECtHR, 8 April 2014).
360. K.D. Ewing and J. Hendy QC, 'The Dramatic Implications of Demir and Baykara'. *Industrial Law Journal* 39:1 (2010): 41.
361. F. Dorssemont, 'How the European Court of Human Rights Gave Us Enerji to Cope with Laval and Viking', in: Marie-Ange Moraeu (ed.), *Before and After the Economic Crisis: What Implications for the 'European Social Model'*, Edward Elgar Publishing Limited. 2014, 217 & 220.
362. For a broader analysis on the literature, *see* C. Stylogiannis, 'The Protection of the Right to Strike under the European Convention on Human Rights'. *UCL Journal of Law and Jurisprudence*, 6:142 (2017) *See also*, K. Arabadjieva, *A Framework for Interpreting the Right to Freedom of Association of Workers and Trade Unions in European Human Rights Law*. PhD Thesis. University of Oxford. 2019.
363. Some of these pre-date Enerji: Karaçay v. Turkey No. 6615/03 (ECtHR, 27 March 2007); Kaya and Seyhan v. Turkey No. 30946/04 (ECtHR, 15 December 2009); Sezer v. Turkey No. 36807/07 (ECtHR, 26 June 2015); Veniamin Tymoshenko v. Ukraine No. 48408/12 (ECtHR, 2 January 2015); Hrvatski Lijecnicki Sindikat v. Croatia No. 36701/09 (ECtHR, 27 February 2015).
364. For example, the case of National Union of Rail, Maritime and Transport Workers v. The United Kingdom cited, where the Court confirmed that strike action is protected by the ECHR, including secondary action. However, it held that the complete ban on secondary action in the UK was compatible with the Convention.

As for the right to bargain collectively, also the analysis of the evolution of the recognition of the right to strike deserves its own chapter, therefore the meaning and the impact of the latest decisions of the Court on this right will be analysed in the third chapter of this section of the volume.

The Strasbourg Court's revirement with respect to the extension of the scope of Article 11 ECHR to the right to strike was seen as a response, in terms of strengthening the protection of collective rights, to the European Court of Justice's Viking, Laval, Ruffert and Luxembourg decisions, in which an 'imbalance' in favour of economic freedoms over trade union rights undoubtedly prevailed.[365] Subsequently, the European Court of Human Rights, in its 2014 Matelly v. France[366] ('Matelly') and Adefdromil v. France[367] ('Adefromil') decisions, found that the *Code de la défense*'s regulations that excluded the right of military personnel to form associations of a trade union nature were incompatible with Article 11 of the Convention. In the aforementioned decisions, the Strasbourg Court recalled the general principles set forth in its own jurisprudence on freedom of trade union association, and in particular the decision Demir and Baykara, recalling that Article 11(1) delineates freedom of trade union association as a special form or aspect of freedom of association.

The ECtHR, in the cases cited above, demonstrates a social sensibility quite different from that expressed by the ECJ in similar cases. In fact, as has been clarified by the doctrine, the balancing act carried out by the Court and the ECJ is structurally different, insofar as the former places the Person as the essential term of comparison, while the latter cannot neglect economic freedoms, which represent the pillars on which the single market was built.[368]

The preceptive content of Article 11 is also supplemented by the provisions of Article 14 regarding the prohibition of discrimination. Freedom of assembly and association as provided for by the ECHR and must therefore be ensured '*without any discrimination, in particular those based on [...] political opinions*'. It follows that whatever instrument adopted by national legislation to guarantee trade union freedom (right to strike, right to information and consultation, right to collective bargaining, etc.), the exercise of the same must be guaranteed in light of the protection of the individual worker's right not to be subjected to discriminatory acts by reason of his or her union choice (or non-choice). This general provision (Article 14) placed at the level of industrial relations tends to counteract those anti-union behaviours actuated by the employer consisting of recognizing more favourable economic treatments overall to non-unionized workers, with the effect of inhibiting and persuading them from joining and participating in unions. Were this not the case, the worker's individual right to protect his or her interests through the union would become evanescent and illusory.

365. F. Dorssemont, 'How the European Court of Human Rights Gave Us Enerji to Cope with Laval and Viking', in: Marie-Ange Moraeu (ed.), *Before and After the Economic Crisis: What Implications for the 'European Social Model'*, Edward Elgar Publishing Limited. 2014, 217 & 220.
366. Case of Matelly v. France No. 10609/10 (ECtHR, 2 October 2014).
367. Case of Adefdromil v. France No. 32191/09 (ECtHR, 2 October 2014).
368. G. Vettori, *Diritti fondamentali e diritti sociali. Una riflessione fra due crisi*, in *Eur. dir. priv.*, n. 3, 2011, p. 640.

The Convention imposes to States both positive and negative responsibilities in order to guarantee the 'effective enjoyment' of the rights granted in itself. While negative responsibilities are self-explanatory since they place a duty on State authorities to refrain from acting in a way that unjustifiably interferes with Convention rights, '*The Court does not have to develop a general theory of the positive obligations which may flow from the Convention.*'[369] As it refuses to give a definition of what should be expected from the States, the Court gives rise to some uncertainly over how far the rights the ECHR provide extend. In the current situation, it is particularly debatable whether Article 11 creates 'duties to promote or fulfil' the rights outlined therein, for example by putting in place a system for collective bargaining.

Many Article 11 cases involve breaches of positive obligations, but these have always involved duties to protect. It was argued in the case of Unite the Union v. The United Kingdom[370] ('Unite') that '*Article 11, interpreted in light of Article 6 of the European Social Charter, required State action to restore both the machinery of collective bargaining on an industry-wide scale and the machinery to enforce collective agreements reached, in order to enable agricultural workers and their union to exercise their right to collective bargaining*', but the Court rejected the argument since '*the European and international instruments to which the applicant referred, as they currently stand, do not support its view that a State's positive obligations under Article 11 extend to providing for a mandatory statutory mechanism for collective bargaining*'. Therefore, a positive obligation does exist; it is recognized by the Court, but what its extent is, is not in any way or shape clear.

6.1 RESTRICTIONS ON MEMBERS OF THE ARMED FORCES, THE POLICE, AND THE STATE ADMINISTRATION

While the State is bound to respect the freedom of assembly and association of its employees, Article 11 § 2 allows it to impose lawful restrictions on the exercise of these rights by members of its armed forces, police or administration (Demir, Tüm Haber Sen and Çınar v. Turkey[371] ('Tüm Haber')).

The term 'lawful' relates to the same idea of lawfulness as that to which other words or phrases in the Convention, most notably 'prescribed by law' contained in the second paragraphs of Articles 9 to 11, refer when they use the same or similar words. In addition to positing compliance with domestic law, the idea of lawfulness utilized in the Convention also entails qualitative criteria in domestic law, such as predictability and, generally, an absence of arbitrariness.

Furthermore, the Court has determined that lawful restrictions placed on members of the armed forces, the police, or the administration of the State must also meet

369. Case of Plattform 'Ärzte Für Das Leben' v. Austria No. 10126/82 (ECtHR, 21 June 1988).
370. Case of Unite the Union v. The United Kingdom No. 65397/13 (ECtHR, 26 May 2016).
371. Case of Tüm Haber Sen and Çınar v. Turkey No. 28602/95 (ECtHR, 21 February 2006). The case concerned the dissolution of a union of public sector workers on the ground that civil servants could not form trade unions. The Court held that there had been a violation of Article 11 of the Convention. It noted in particular that the 'State as employer' must respect trade union freedom and guarantee its effective exercise.

a critical social need and be 'necessary in a democratic society' (Tüm Haber; Adefdromil; Trade Union of the Police in the Slovak Republic and Others v. Slovakia[372]) even though the requirement of necessity is not specifically mentioned in Article 11.

Therefore, while the idea of trade-union freedom may be consistent with the restriction on the right to strike for some types of public employees, an outright ban on the formation of unions imposed on government officials is incompatible with Article 11 (Tüm Haber; Demir). Moreover, this prohibition does not apply to all public workers or staff members of state-run businesses or industries (Enerji; Junta Rectora Del Ertzainen Nazional Elkartasuna (ER.N.E.) v. Spain[373] ('Junta Rectora')).

In light of the special responsibilities entrusted to the police force and the probable repercussions of interrupting its operations, the prohibition on strike action imposed on a police trade union pursues the legitimate goal of avoiding unrest. The limitation of the police's freedom to organize is justified by the necessity for them to provide a constant service and the fact that they are armed, which sets them apart from other government workers. In order to govern specific parts of a police trade union's operations in the public interest, the State is given a sufficiently large margin of appreciation; nonetheless, this does not mean that the union will lose the essence of its rights under Article 11 (Junta Rectora).

The Court has accepted that trade-union activity has to be adapted to take into account the specific nature of the armed forces' mission and that even significant restrictions can be imposed on the forms of action and expression of an occupational association and its members. However, such restrictions should not deprive them of the general right of association to defend their occupational and non-pecuniary interests (Adefdromil; Matelly). A blanket ban on forming or joining a trade union by military personnel encroaches on the very essence of their freedom of association and is as such prohibited by the Convention (Adefdromil; Matelly).

6.2 A PATH FORWARD: CHOICES FOR THE FUTURE

The right of association includes the following essential elements: (1) the right to form or join a trade union, (2) the prohibition of closed-shop agreements, (3) the right for a

372. Case of Trade Union of the Police in the Slovak Republic and Others v. Slovakia No. 11828/08 (ECtHR, 25 September 2012).
373. Case of Junta Rectora Del Ertzainen Nazional Elkartasuna (ER.N.E.) v. Spain No. 45892/09 (ECtHR, 21 April 2015). In Junta Rectora, the Court considered the appeal of the Police union, which argued that the legal prohibition of the right to strike in relation to Police unions violated their freedom of association. The Court had already had the opportunity to interpret the exceptions provided in the second part of Article 11. Thus, in Matelly and Adefdromil cases, it held that restrictions on the right to organize imposed on military personnel should not undermine the very essence of this right and held that the blanket exclusion of military personnel's right to form and join a union violated Article 11. In Junta Rectora, the Court delimited the scope of any restrictions on the right of Police unions to organize. The Court noted that the restriction in question was spread only on members of the State Security Forces Corps as guarantors of public safety and not on all public employees as, e.g., in Enerji. It also stressed that states enjoy a wide margin of appreciation in providing for the scope of police officers' union rights. Limitations on such rights are justified by a special character of the Police, which should provide uninterrupted service in the sphere of public safety. Based on these considerations, the Court justified the ban on strikes against Police officers.

trade union to seek to persuade the employer to hear what it has to say on behalf of its members and, in principle, (4) the right to bargain collectively with the employer (Demir; Sindicatul 'Păstorul cel Bun' v. Romania[374] ('Pastorul cel Bun')). This list is non-exhaustive and subject to evolution depending on particular developments in labour relations.

In its evolution, the Court has been taking and will continue to take into account elements of international law other than the Convention, the interpretation of such elements by competent organs, and the practice of European States reflecting their common values (Demir; Manole and 'Romanian Farmers Direct' v. Romania[375] ('Manole')). Besides, it would be inconsistent with its methods and its purposes for the Court to adopt, in relation to Article 11, an interpretation of the scope of freedom of association of trade unions that is much narrower than that which prevails in international law (National Union of Rail, Maritime and Transport Workers v. The United Kingdom[376] ('RMT')).

Two principles guide the Court's approach to the substance of the right of association; first, the Court takes into consideration the totality of the measures taken by the State concerned in order to secure trade-union freedom, subject to its margin of appreciation; second, the Court does not accept restrictions that affect the essential elements of trade-union freedom, without which that freedom would become devoid of substance. While in principle States are free to decide what measures they wish to take in order to ensure compliance with Article 11, they are under an obligation to take account of the elements regarded as essential by the Court's case law (Demir).

Even when implementing their obligations under EU or European Economic Area (EEA) law, contracting parties should ensure that restrictions imposed on Article 11 rights do not affect the essential elements of trade union freedom, without which that freedom would become devoid of substance (Norwegian Confederation of Trade Unions (LO) and Norwegian Transport Workers' Union (NTF) v. Norway[377] ('Holship')).

While the collective dimension of Article 11 has significantly expanded in the last period, beginning with Wilson, National Union of Journalists and Others v. The United Kingdom[378] ('Wilson'), where the Court found that by permitting employers to use financial incentives to induce employees to surrender important union rights, the respondent State *failed in its positive obligation* to *secure the enjoyment of the rights*

374. Case of Sindicatul 'Păstorul Cel Bun' v. Romania No. 2330/09 (ECtHR, 9 July 2013).
375. Case of Manole and 'Romanian Farmers Direct' v. Romania No. 46551/06 (ECtHR, 16 June 2015).
376. Case of National Union of Rail, Maritime and Transport Workers v. The United Kingdom No. 31045/10 (ECtHR, 8 April 2014).
377. Case of Norwegian Confederation of Trade Unions (LO) and Norwegian Transport Workers' Union (NTF) v. Norway No. 45487/17 (ECtHR, 10 June 2021).
378. Case of Wilson, National Union of Journalists and Others v. The United Kingdom Nos 30668/96, 30671/96 and 30678/96 (ECtHR, 2 July 2002).

under Article 11, there are a lot of ways in which the Court could be found lacking, in comparison with other international instruments, such as ILO or ESC norms.[379]

An answer to why the Court appears so reticent to open its wings and take flight in the matter of labour rights, as someone would hope, could be found in the concurring opinion of judge Wojtyczek in the case of RMT: '*To conclude, in my view, the analysis of international law does not support the opinion that Article 11 of the Convention should be interpreted in such a way as to encompass the right to sympathy strikes. To hold otherwise exposes the Court to the risk of being legitimately criticised for judicial activism.*'

The Court reads the political humus in which it lives and tries not to go against the political currents to not undermine its standing among all the States.

This humus brings out a question: how will the plant grow? What's the path forward?

As it is, the right to freedom of association has long been recognized and protected by Conventions 87[380] and 98[381] of the International Labour Organisation (ILO),[382] as well as Articles 5 and 6 of the ESC. The ECHR has only more recently sprouted as a source of protection of collective labour rights.[383]

In both normative systems - ILO and ESC - the right to freedom of association is a right which encloses different sub-rights, including a right to collective bargaining and the right to take collective action, as to secure to any organization the possibility to act in a way which could indeed be effective in the defence of their social and economic interests.

Under both systems, the rights discussed here are of significant substance, and seek to provide a high (minimum) level of protection.[384]

However, there have been significant concerns over the effectiveness of the enforcement mechanisms of both systems. These are primarily based on ongoing

379. *See*, among others, A. Perulli and V. Brino, *Handbook of International Labour Law, e-Book*, Giappichelli Editore, 2018.
380. Freedom of Association and Protection of the Right to Organise Convention 1948 (No. 87).
381. Right to Organise and Collective Bargaining Convention 1949 (No. 98).
382. There are further Conventions related to the right to freedom of association of specific categories of workers, such as the Labour Relations (Public Service) Convention 1978 (No. 151) or Rural Workers' Organisations Convention 1975 (No. 141), which will not be considered here.
383. The ILO is a global organization founded in 1919 in the wake of World War I, concerned specifically with the protection of labour rights. *See* G. Rodgers, E. Lee, L. Swepston, J. an Daele, *The International Labour Organization and the Quest for Social Justice, 1919-2009* (International Labour Office 2009).

    Social justice and fair competition are themes which emerge most clearly as the original driving forces behind the establishment of the organization. The ESC is a Council of Europe instrument originally adopted in 1961 which protects a series of social and economic rights, and is the sister instrument of the ECHR. The Council of Europe was established in 1949 as a reaction to the events of World War II, and is a regional organization with broader political and social aims than the ILO.
384. *See ILO Compilation of decisions of the Committee on Freedom of Association* (6th ed., 2018); *see also* Council of Europe, *Digest of the case-law of the European Committee of Social Rights* (Strasbourg, June 2022).

review and dialogue, cooperation,[385] and, ultimately, political peer pressure to ensure compliance.[386]

In theory, the expansion of the ECHR offers a chance to improve the defence of collective labour rights among Council of Europe Member States, and this is primarily due to the fact that the ECHR is supported by much stronger enforcement measures than the ILO and ESC provisions. It is not without issues though. Recent European Court of Human Rights case law reveals points of divergence and conflict between norms, suggesting that the level of protection under the ECHR may occasionally be lower than under parallel ILO and ESC guarantees - even where the same rights are recognized as protected under all of the instruments.

There's a particular concern arising from this development, namely that ECHR norms that diverge from and conflict with ILO and ESC freedom of association guarantees could displace and undermine the authority of the latter, specialist mechanisms, which provide an overall higher level of protection.

Of course, this issue may be significantly reduced by interpreting the ECHR's freedom of association protections in a manner that is more in line with ILO and ESC standards.

The ILO and ESC standards should therefore be the Court's primary sources of authority when interpreting the ECHR's rights of freedom of association, and any diverging interpretation of these standards must be supported on the basis of appropriate reasons. As it will be shown in the following chapters, a lot of the 'steps forward' done by the ECtHR were done by referencing international principles. Therefore the 'social frigidity' of the Court on the recognition of, e.g., the right to strike appears even more evident and alarming.

385. *See*, e.g., *ILO Compilation of decisions of the Committee on Freedom of Association* (n 22) [5]: '*The object of the special procedure on freedom of association is not to blame or punish anyone, but rather to engage in a constructive tripartite dialogue to promote respect for trade union rights in law and practice.*'

386. Compliance with Conventions is assessed mainly by the Committee of Experts on the Application of Conventions and Recommendations (CEACR), and the Committee on Freedom of Association (CFA). The conclusions of the CFA and CEACR are not legally binding, the explicit competence to interpret ILO Conventions being reserved for the International Court of Justice: ILO Constitution Article 37. However, only one case has ever been brought to the ICJ and the pronouncements of these Committees have been regarded as authoritative and respected.

CHAPTER 7

The Right to Collective Bargaining

As stated above, in the Demir case of 2008, the Court reevaluated its prior precedent holding that the ability to collectively bargain and to enter into agreements was not a necessary element of Article 11 and was not required in order to effectively exercise trade union freedom.

It held that the right to bargain collectively with the employer had, in principle, become one of the essential components of the '*right to form and to join trade unions for the protection of [one's] interests*' set forth in Article 11 of the Convention, with the understanding that States remained free to organize their system so as, if appropriate, to grant special status to collective bargaining agreements with employers.

Having had regard to the developments in labour law and to the practice of contracting States in such matters, Demir represented a more than significant step towards bringing ECtHR jurisprudence in line with ILO and ESC standards, since these instruments were crucial to this development. In a significant paragraph, the Court held that:

> The Court, in defining the meaning of terms and notions in the text of the Convention, can and must take into account elements of international law other than the Convention, the interpretation of such elements by competent organs, and the practice of European states reflecting their common values. The consensus emerging from specialized international instruments and from the practice of contracting states may constitute a relevant consideration for the Court when it interprets the provisions of the Convention in specific cases. In this context, it is not necessary for the respondent State to have ratified the entire collection of instruments that are applicable in respect of the precise subject matter of the case concerned. It will be sufficient for the Court that the relevant international instruments denote a continuous evolution in the norms and principles applied in international law or in the domestic law of the majority of Member States of the Council of Europe and show, in a precise area, that there is common ground in modern societies.[387]

387. Demir case, paras 85-86.

The Court, therefore, took into account, among others, ILO and ESC instruments and their interpretation in recognizing a right to collective bargaining. However, as it was made clear by subsequent decisions, the right to collective bargaining under Article 11 is very far from equivalent in substance to what ILO and ESC guarantee.

As it is, the Court in RMT stated that Demir involved 'a very far-reaching interference with freedom of association, one that intruded into its inner core, namely the dissolution of a trade union'. Thus, the Court took a step back, stating that Demir was an extreme case which effectively involved a complete denial of the right to form trade unions and to bargain collectively, making it very difficult to argue that this was not a violation of Article 11.

7.1 OBJECTIVE LIMITATIONS TO THE RIGHT OF COLLECTIVE BARGAINING

It stands that the right to collective bargaining has many objective limitations that have been construed and delimited by the Court over the course of the years. For example, it cannot and has not ever been interpreted as including a 'right' to a collective agreement or a right for a trade union to maintain a collective agreement on a particular matter for an indefinite period, such as in the Swedish Transport Workers Union v. Sweden[388] case.

In this case, the applicant trade union complained of the refusal of the National Collective Bargaining Office to conclude a collective agreement with it, although it had concluded such agreements with the main trade union federations and sometimes with independent trade unions, no violation of Article 11 of the Convention was found by the Court: the Office's general policy of restricting the number of organizations with which it concluded collective agreements was not in itself incompatible with trade union freedom and fell within the State's margin of appreciation. Article 11 did not secure any particular treatment of trade unions such as the right to conclude collective agreements.

Also, there is no requirement under the Convention that an employer enters into, or remains in, any particular collective bargaining arrangement or accede to the requests of a union on behalf of its members (UNISON v. the United Kingdom[389] ('UNISON')). More recently, in Association of Civil Servants and Union for Collective Bargaining and Others v. Germany,[390] the Court considered that the national legislation, rendering conflicting collective agreements concluded by minority trade unions

388. Case of Swedish Transport Workers' Union v. Sweden No. 53507/99 (ECtHR, 30 November 2004).

389. Case of UNISON v. The United Kingdom No. 53574/99 (ECtHR, 10 January 2002). In this case the court stated that *'[w]hile Article 11 includes trade union freedom as a specific aspect of freedom of association, it does not secure any particular treatment of trade union members by the State. There is no express inclusion of a right to strike or an obligation on employers to engage in collective bargaining. At most, Article 11 may be regarded as safeguarding the freedom of trade unions to protect the occupational interests of their members'*.

390. Case of Association of Civil Servants and Union for Collective Bargaining and Others v. Germany Nos 815/18, 3278/18, 12380/18, 12693/18 and 14883/18 (ECtHR, 5 July 2022).

inapplicable, did not breach Article 11, having regard to the respondent State's margin of appreciation in the area, the limited scope of the restriction and the weighty aim of securing the proper functioning of the system of collective bargaining in the interests of both employees and employers.

This case concerned the Uniformity of Collective Agreements Act, which regulates conflicts that arise if there are several collective agreements in one 'business unit' of a company. The applicants – three German trade unions and six members of one of them – submitted that the relevant provisions of the Act in question had violated their right to form and join trade unions, including the right to collective bargaining. They argued in particular that the legislation had resulted in their not being able to conclude collective agreements in companies in which a different trade union had more members, and in employers no longer wishing to negotiate with them.

The Court held that there had been no violation of Article 11 of the Convention, finding that there had been no disproportionate restriction on the applicants' rights in the present case. The Court reiterated in particular that the right to collective bargaining as guaranteed under Article 11 of the Convention did not include a 'right' to a collective agreement. What was essential was that trade unions could make representations to and be heard by employers. In this case, the Court found that the restrictions brought on by the legislation had concerned smaller trade unions, which nonetheless retained other rights, including the right to collective bargaining and to strike. Moreover, the legislation was intended to ensure the proper functioning of the collective bargaining system in the interests of both employees and employers.

7.2 SUBJECTIVE LIMITATIONS TO THE RIGHT OF COLLECTIVE BARGAINING

On the matter of subjective limitations to access to the right to bargain collectively it could be argued that the real issue is actually the scope of trade union rights. As already discussed, Article 11 presents trade-union freedom only as one form or a special aspect of freedom of association, not as an independent right (Belgian Police). Therefore, the elements of the freedom of association outlined above as well as the conditions for interfering with that freedom apply equally to trade unions. Thus, trade-union freedom is an essential element of social dialogue between workers and employers, and hence an important tool in achieving social justice and harmony (Pastorul cel Bun).

Article 11 safeguards freedom to protect the occupational interests of trade-union members by trade-union action, the conduct and development of which the contracting States must both permit and make possible (Swedish Engine Drivers' Union case, Tüm Haber). However, the words '*for the protection of his interests*' cannot be construed as meaning that only individuals and not trade unions may make a complaint under this provision (Federation of Offshore Workers' Trade Unions and Others v. Norway[391]

391. Case of Federation of Offshore Workers' Trade Unions and Others v. Norway No. 38190/97 (ECtHR, 27 June 2002).

('Offshore Workers')) since Article 11 protects both workers and unions (Yakut Republican Trade-Union Federation v. Russia[392] ('Yakut')).

Bearing in mind what the scope of trade union rights is, it can be said that Article 11 § 2 does not exclude any occupational group from the scope of the article, but (and here's the theme of this paragraph) the national authorities are indeed entitled to impose '*lawful restrictions*' on certain of their employees in accordance with Article 11 § 2. Article 11 thus can be said to technically apply to everyone in an employment relationship, granting to every single group access to the right to bargain collectively.

On this matter, three specific cases could assist in the comprehension of what can amount to 'lawful restriction'.

In the case of Sindicatul 'Păstorul cel Bun' v. Romania, concerning members of the clergy, the Romanian State refused the application for registration of a trade union formed by priests of the Romanian Orthodox Church. The Grand Chamber held that '*members of the clergy fulfil their mission in the context of an employment relationship falling within the scope of Article 11 of the Convention. Article 11 is therefore applicable to the facts of the case*'[393] but there had been no violation of Article 11 of the Convention. This was done by finding that in refusing to register the applicant union, the State had simply declined to become involved in the organization and operation of the Romanian Orthodox Church, thereby observing its duty of denominational neutrality under Article 9 (freedom of thought, conscience and religion) of the Convention. In the Grand Chamber's view, the court's refusal to register the union for failure to comply with the requirement of obtaining the archbishop's permission was a direct consequence of the right of the religious community concerned to make its own organizational arrangements and to operate in accordance with the provisions of its own Statute.

Following up, in Manole's[394] case, regarding self-employed farmers and, again, the refusal of the Romanian courts to register a union of self-employed farmers which the first applicant wished to set up.

The Court held that there had been no violation of Article 11 of the Convention, finding that the refusal to register the applicant union had not overstepped the Romanian authorities' margin of appreciation as to the manner in which they secured the right of freedom of association to self-employed farmers.

The Court, therefore, found that Romanian Courts pursued a legitimate aim in denying the registration, namely to safeguard the economic and social order by maintaining a distinction between trade unions and other kinds of associations.[395] The legislation in force at the time of the events, like that currently in force, had in no way restricted the applicants' right to form professional associations. Moreover, the Court had no evidence in the present case to suggest that, if the persons concerned were to

392. Case of Yakut Republican Trade-Union Federation v. Russia No. 29582/09 (ECtHR, 7 December 2021).
393. Pastorul cel Bun case, para. 148.
394. Case of Manole and 'Romanian Farmers Direct' v. Romania, cited (33).
395. It's not a core matter of this volume, but it should be noted that there is a fundamental difference between Trade Unions and Trade Associations and that the Court stood by it in this decision.

form an association, it would lack the essential prerogatives enabling it to defend the collective interests of its members in dealings with the public authorities.

In sum, the refusal to register the applicants as a trade union had not overstepped the national authorities' margin of appreciation in this sphere and had therefore not been disproportionate.

Lastly, in 2021, another important judgment was delivered which could very well be called a key case for the importance of the contribution to the development of the Court's case law. This is the case of Yakut Republican Trade-Union Federation v. Russia, which regarded a trade-union federation ordered to expel a grassroots union of working prisoners because of a statutory ban on their unionization and which was found in no violation of Article 11.

As stated, Article 11 protects both workers and unions and as a worker should be free to join a union, so should the union be free to choose its members. By extension, as a union should be free to join a federation, so should the federation be free to admit the union.

The court order, which obliged the applicant federation to expel the trade union, had restricted the applicant's right under Article 11, but that restriction had been prescribed by law, since like prisoners' other Convention rights, their right to form and to join trade unions could be restricted for security, in particular, for the prevention of crime and disorder.

Although the Convention does not precisely define the concept of 'trade union' beyond a general indication that it's an association formed for the purpose of defending the interests of its members, most of the cases considered by the Court concern employees and, more broadly, persons in an 'employment relationship'.

However, prison work could not be equated with employment. Indeed, prison work differs from the work performed by ordinary employees in many aspects. It serves the primary aim of rehabilitation and resocialization, is aimed at reintegration, and is obligatory.[396] A similar view had been expressed by the Russian Constitutional Court.

While it is true that prisoners in general continue to enjoy all the fundamental rights and freedoms guaranteed under the Convention save for the right to liberty, trade-union freedom might be difficult to exercise in detention.

Nevertheless, the Convention is a 'living instrument' and it might well be, therefore, that developments in that field might at some point in future necessitate the extension of the trade-union freedom to working inmates, especially if they worked for a private employer. Indeed, paragraph 2 of Article 11 did not exclude any occupational group from the scope of that Article.

However, having regard to the current practice of the member States of the Council of Europe, there was no sufficient consensus to give Article 11 the interpretation advocated by the applicant.

396. On the matter, it should be remembered that Article 4 of the Convention, which concerns the prohibition of slavery and forced labour, does not apply to forced labour in prison.

7.3 A POSITIVE OBLIGATION

As already mentioned before, there are no State's positive obligations under Article 11 to provide for a mandatory statutory mechanism for collective bargaining (Unite; Wilson).

However, genuine and effective respect for freedom of association cannot be reduced to a mere duty on the part of the State not to interfere (Ouranio Toxo and Others v. Greece[397]). The national authorities may in certain circumstances be obliged to intervene in the relationship between private individuals by taking reasonable and appropriate measures to secure the effective enjoyment of the right to freedom of association (Wilson).

Whether the case is analysed in terms of a positive duty on the State or in terms of interference by a public authority which needs to be justified, the criteria to be applied do not differ in substance. In both contexts, regard must be had to the fair balance to be struck between the competing interests of the individual and of the community as a whole (Sørensen).

Two recent cases of the Court dealt with the matter of positive obligation of the contracting States under article 11 with reference to the right to bargain collectively. In 2016, in the case of Unite the Union v. United Kingdom,[398] which was about the alleged inability of trade unions to engage in collective bargaining owing to the abolition of the relevant wages council, the Court found the applicant's reasons lacking and pronounced an inadmissibility decision.

The case stemmed from a series of consultations with interested parties, including the applicant – a trade union representing around 18,000 employees in the agricultural sector – following which the UK Government succeeded in having adopted new legal provisions abolishing the Agricultural Wages Board (AWB) for England and Wales, a statutory body which for many years had set minimum wages and conditions in the agricultural sector. The Board comprised among its members' representatives of employers and employees, the latter being nominated most recently by the applicant. The applicant argued that the abolition of the Board infringed on its right to engage in collective bargaining in the interests of its members, being an essential element of the right to form and join a trade union.

The case concerned the extent of the United Kingdom's positive obligation under Article 11, in particular, whether it was obliged to have in place a mandatory, statutory forum for collective bargaining in the agricultural sector. In this sphere and in the absence of an established consensus among the Member States of the Council of Europe, the respondent State enjoyed a wide margin of appreciation in determining whether a fair balance was struck between the protection of the public interest in the abolition of the AWB and the applicant's competing rights under Article 11.

This would seem like an important, even catastrophic step back from what was stated in Demir in 2008, but there's a different context which has to be taken into consideration.

397. Case of Ouranio Toxo and Others v. Greece No. 74989/01 (ECtHR, 20 October 2005).
398. Case of Unite the Union v. The United Kingdom, cited (28).

The abolition of the AWB was preceded by research into pay and conditions in the agricultural sector and a public consultation. The consultation paper put forward a number of reasons tending to support the AWB's abolition, all of which were relevant to the decision where the balance between the competing interests lies. In particular, it was noted that the AWB was the only outstanding wage council and that there were indications that a number of agricultural workers were already negotiating their own agreements. The financial implications of abolition on workers and farmers and the net savings in terms of the AWB's operating costs were assessed. The human rights implications of the proposal had also been considered.

Significantly, the applicant had not been prevented from engaging in collective bargaining. The conditions for collective agreements to be deemed to be legally enforceable in the United Kingdom - the existence of intent to be bound by the collective agreement and of an agreement in writing - did not appear unreasonable or unduly restrictive. The applicant remained free to take steps to protect the operational interests of its members by collective action, including collective bargaining, and by engaging in negotiations to seek to persuade employers and employees to reach collective agreements and it had the right to be heard.

Therefore, it could not be said that the United Kingdom Parliament lacked relevant and sufficient reasons for enacting the contested legislation or that the abolition of the AWB had failed to strike a fair balance between the competing interests at stake.

The following year, in 2017 another case went beyond merely applying existing case law on the matter of positive obligations by the contracting States on the matter of the right to Collective Bargain, positioning itself in between Demir and Unite cases.

This is the case of Tek Gıda İş Sendikası v. Turkey,[399] which regarded both the refusal, based on statute, to recognize trade unions as representing staff and the large-scale dismissals of trade-union members resulting in the absence of union representation for company employees. While the first item was found not in violation of the ECHR, the second found all the Judges in agreement for a Judgment of violation.

The applicant complained, in particular, about the domestic courts' refusal to recognize its representation as a precondition for collective bargaining within a company, which the union submitted had been a result of an erroneous calculation of the number of union members on the staff of the company.

In May 2004, the total membership of the applicant trade union had been sufficient for it to be recognized by the Ministry of Labour and Social Security as capable of representing employees in collective bargaining under the 'majority of the company employees' criterion. The company, however, contested that recognition demonstrating that the applicant trade union did not have enough members, the Labour Court upheld the company's challenge and the trade union appealed, unsuccessfully.

According to well-established case law, the States have a wide margin of appreciation in determining the conditions for the recognition of a trade union as

399. Case of Tek Gıda Iş Sendikası v. Turkey No. 35009/05 (ECtHR, 4 April 2017).

representative. The ECtHR researched the application by national courts of the rule according to which the union has to unite at least half of the total number of employees of the enterprise in order to be acknowledged as representative. Such a stipulation, in the opinion of the ECtHR, did not affect the right of the trade union to seek to persuade the employer by means other than collective bargaining. Therefore the decisions of the court did not affect the very heart of the trade union's activity and did not violate Article 11.

Subsequently, the company dismissed the forty employees who were members of the applicant trade union on redundancies or for professional shortcomings. Those former employees appealed to the Labour Courts on grounds of wrongful dismissal and requested their reinstatement in post.

Turkey's labour courts found in favour of the dismissed employees, considering that they had been dismissed on the grounds of their membership of a trade union. The courts ordered the company to reinstate them, or else to pay each of them compensation for wrongful dismissal equivalent to one year's wages. The company did not reinstate any of them, deciding to pay.

This resulted in trade union no longer having any members among the staff of that company.

The Court was very rigorous in its evaluation of the Turkish law which did not provide for reinstatement as an obligatory remedy in such cases, and the decisions of the courts, permitting the payment of compensation instead of reinstatement. It found that non-reinstatement of unlawfully dismissed trade union members resulted in the loss by the applicant union of its members and had a discouraging effect on the other employees as regards their membership of the applicant union.

The Court pointed out that the latter had thus lost its chances of keeping its members or attracting new members and reaching the threshold of representativeness essential for negotiating collective agreements. Based on these conclusions the ECtHR found that permitting the choice of the employer to pay compensation instead of reinstating the dismissed employees resulted in the de-unionization of all employees and the loss by the applicant union of its members.

Consequently, neither the legislature nor the courts involved in the case had fulfilled their positive obligation to guarantee the applicant trade union's effective enjoyment of its right to attempt to convince the employer to listen to its comments on behalf of its members and, in principle, of its right to collectively bargain with it. It followed that the requisite fair balance had not been struck between the competing interests of the applicant trade union and the company as a whole.

7.4 POSSIBILITY: THE DOOR TO THE FUTURE IS OPEN OR CLOSED?

The essence of a voluntary system of collective bargaining, in the view of the ECtHR, is that *it must only be possible* for a trade union – even if not recognized by an employer – to take steps including, if necessary, organizing industrial action, with a view to persuading the employer to enter into collective bargaining with it on those issues which the union believes are important for its members' interests (Wilson).

Between the many objective and subjective limitations that the Court in its decisions through the years has been continually delineating and precising, a positive obligation of the contracting States does exist to assure that it is indeed possible for its citizens and trade unions to bargain collectively, but no other more profound obligation can be found in the jurisprudence of the Court or in the letter of the article. To cite the Court's own words '*At most, Article 11 may be regarded as safeguarding the freedom of trade unions to protect the occupational interests of their members.*'[400] It does not get better than that.

400. Case of UNISON v. The United Kingdom, (40).

CHAPTER 8

The Right to Strike

No better words to start a chapter on the right to strike could be used than those of Ewing and Hendy: 'in the absence of the right to strike, the right to collective bargain is no more than a right to collective begging'.[401]

As was already indicated, the ECHR has been viewed as a tool for upholding principally civil and political rights. Even though the Council of Europe's official position is based on the idea that human rights are interdependent, indivisible, and interrelated, Tonia Novitz noted a '*disparity between this rhetorical claim and the actual reality*'[402] with regard to the protection of socioeconomic rights, particularly the right to strike.

8.1 GENERAL APPROACH TO THE RIGHT TO STRIKE

The Court in a number of cases during the 1970s adopted a rather restrictive interpretation, by merely emphasizing that Article 11 imposes a duty on contracting states to provide mechanisms that allow trade unions to represent their members; it did not make any particular reference to the methods by which this was to be done.[403] As a result, the Court rejected the arguments made by trade unions to protect their interests in relation to the rights to group bargaining, consultation, and strike.[404]

401. Ewing K.D., Hendy QC J. 'The Dramatic Implications of Demir and Baykara'. *Industrial Law Journal* 39 (2010).
402. T. Novitz, *International and European Protection of the Right to Strike: A Comparative Study of Standards Set by the International Labour Organization, the Council of Europe and the European Union*. Oxford University Press, Oxford 2013, 180.
403. *See* M. Forde, 'The European Convention on Human Rights and Labor Law'. *The American Journal of Comparative Law* 31 (1983): 301-332. For an excursus on the most relevant jurisprudence, *see also* G. Raimondi, *Il diritto di sciopero è elemento essenziale della libertà di associazione? Evoluzione della giurisprudenza della Corte europea dei diritti dell'uomo, in* Lavoro, Diritti, Europa 2019 / 1.
404. *See also* the case of Swedish Engine Drivers' Union v. Sweden No. 5614/72 (ECtHR, 6 February 1976).

One of the cases that opened the new approach of the European Court of Human Rights to recognize the right to strike as being protected under Article 11, was not about strike per se. In 1991, in the case Ezelin v. France,[405] the Court found itself evaluating a disciplinary penalty imposed on the applicant, a member of a Trade Union, for taking part in a public demonstration. The penalty was found to be in violation of Article 11 of the Convention: although the penalty had mainly moral force, the Court considered that '*the freedom to take part in a peaceful assembly – in this instance a demonstration that had not been prohibited – is of such importance that it cannot be restricted in any way, even for an avocat, so long as the person concerned does not himself commit any reprehensible act on such an occasion*'.

This first rock in the pond brought then the Court to the Wilson case of 2002, where the Court noted in particular that '[t]he essence of a voluntary system of collective bargaining is that it must be possible for a trade union which is not recognised by an employer to take steps including, if necessary, *organising industrial action*, with a view to persuading the employer to enter into collective bargaining with it on those issues which the union believes are important for its members' interests'.

Since then, the right to strike has come to represent one of the most important means by which the State may secure a trade union's freedom to protect its members' occupational interests (Schmidt and Dahlström; Wilson), but this right is not absolute and may very well be subject to regulation under national law (Enerji). Therefore, restrictions imposed by a contracting State on the exercise of the right to strike do not in themselves give rise to an issue under Article 11 of the Convention (Offshore Workers).

While on one hand, some cases involve relatively extreme restrictions, such as the government circular banning strike action, on the other, others have involved less extreme sanctions capable of dissuading workers from taking part in strike action.

Although the right to take strike action has not yet been considered an essential element of trade union freedom,[406] strike action is clearly protected by Article 11 (Association of Academics v. Iceland;[407] RMT) and the Court has referred to a strike as the most powerful instrument available to a trade union to protect the occupational

405. Case of Ezelin v. France No. 11800/85 (ECtHR, 26 April 1991).

406. It not surprising that the Enerji ruling was initially interpreted to have implicitly recognized the right to strike as an essential element of trade union freedom protected by Article 11 of the Convention within the framework of collective bargaining. However, since the beginning, this view was not unanimous. In the 31 July 2009 decision of the Court of Appeal for England and Wales in Metrobus Ltd v. Unite the Union, Lord Justice Lloyd expressed himself as follows: '*The contrast between the full and explicit judgment of the Grand Chamber in Demir and Baykara on the one hand, and the more summary discussion of the point in Enerji Yapi-Yol Sen on the other is quite noticeable. It does not seem to me that it would be prudent to proceed on the basis that the less fully articulated judgment in the latter case has developed the Court's case-law by the discrete further stage of recognising a right to take industrial action as an essential element in the rights afforded by article 11.*' Hence came RMT, where the Court put Enerji on the same level as Demir, which declared the right to strike merely as 'important' and not 'essential': '*The Court does not discern any need in the present case to determine whether the taking of industrial action should now be accorded the status of an essential element of the Article 11 guarantee.*'

407. Case of Association of Academics v. Iceland No. 2451/16 (ECtHR, 15 May 2018). In this case, the applicant trade union, represented 18 of its member unions, many in the healthcare sector,

interests of its members (Hrvatski liječnički Sindikat v. Croatia[408] ('Hrvatski')), even going so far as including secondary action, a strike action against a different employer aimed at exerting indirect pressure on the employer involved in the industrial dispute (RMT).

It did so by reference to ILO[409] and ESC norms, resisting the Government's objections to the existence of a right to strike under Convention 87. However, the ECtHR held that the complete ban on secondary action in the UK was compatible with the Convention: such a ban was within the (wide) margin of appreciation of the state and did not strike at the very core of trade union freedom because secondary action was 'accessory' industrial action. It is unclear then to what extent Article 11 does protect a right to strike, for practical purposes, if a complete ban on secondary action does not strike at the substance of the right.

That said, RMT gives rise to uncertainty over how far the Court is willing to extend protection. Only one thing is crystal clear: strike action is, in principle, protected by Article 11 only in so far as it is called by trade-union organizations and considered as being effectively – and not merely presumed to be – part of the trade-union activity (Barış and Others v. Turkey[410] ('Barış')).

So, since the prohibition of a strike must be regarded as a restriction on the trade union's power to protect the interests of its members and thus discloses a restriction on the freedom of association (UNISON; Hrvatski; Veniamin Tymoshenko and Others v. Ukraine[411]), while restrictions may be imposed on the right to strike of workers providing essential services to the population, a complete ban requires solid reasons from the State to justify its necessity (Ognevenko v. Russia[412] ('Ognevenko'); Offshore Workers) and the impact of any restriction on unions' ability to take strike action must not place their members at any real or immediate risk of detriment or of being left defenceless against future attempts to downgrade pay or other work conditions (UNISON).

---

argued that the restriction on the right to strike during the process of collective bargaining and the introduction of compulsory arbitration in the Law adopted in 2015, violated their freedom of association.

The ECtHR pointed that domestic courts have rightly taken into account the effects of the strike on the healthcare sector, and concluded that the impugned measures could be regarded as 'necessary in a democratic society'. It traditionally noted that the right to strike is not absolute (*see also* Junta Rectora case, para. 33; Enerji case, para. 32) and pointed that the member unions had in fact been able to exercise two of the essential elements of freedom of association: the right to seek to persuade the employer to hear what it had to say and the right to engage in collective bargaining. On these grounds the Court agreed with the overall assessment the application by the Icelandic court and declared the application inadmissible.

408. Case of Hrvatski Liječnički Sindikat v. Croatia No. 36701/09 (ECtHR, 27 November 2014).
409. *See* V.F. Ebert and M. Oelz, 'Bridging the Gap Between Labour Rights and Human Rights: The Role of ILO Law in Regional Human Rights Courts', IILS Discussion paper DP/2/212/2012, ILO, Geneve, 2012; *see also* K. Ewing, 'United Kingdom', in: C. LA Macchia (ed.), *The Right to Strike in the EU, The Complexity of the Norms and Safeguarding Efficacy*, Ediesse 2011.
410. Case of Bariş and Others v. Turkey No. 66828/16, 68492/16, 68886/16 et al. (ECtHR, 14 December 2021).
411. Case of Veniamin Tymoshenko and Others v. Ukraine No. 48408/12 (ECtHR, 2 October 2014).
412. Case of Ognevenko v. Russia No. 44873/09 (ECtHR, 20 November 2018).

8.2 Recent Case Law on the Right to Strike

The more recent Ognevenko case contrasts with RMT also in certain methodological aspects. The case concerned the dismissal of a locomotive driver employed by Russian Railways for his participation in strike action. Russian legislation prohibited strikes of railway workers responsible for the circulation of trains. The case concerned the dismissal of a train driver who took part in a strike as Russian law expressly prohibited the strike for railway staff. The ECtHR has considered the relevant national rules, international law, and the jurisprudence of human rights bodies and found out that the Russian norms banning the right to strike for railway staff do not correspond to international standards. The Court was reluctant to find that railway was an essential service and referred to ILO's and ECSR's conclusions in this respect. The ECtHR noted that the trade union notified the Russian Railways of the strike in advance and it was not declared illegal by Russian courts. It also stated that the dismissal as a sanction had a 'chilling effect' on trade union members taking part in industrial actions. These findings led the ECtHR to the conclusion that the dismissal constituted a disproportionate restriction of the applicant's right to freedom of association and violated Article 11 of the ECHR. It should be underlined that the Court did not mention that the ban itself amounted to a violation of the ECHR and was a disproportionate measure; however, this stance might be read between the lines.

Therefore, this decision is of significant interest to labour law scholars as it represents the dialogue between different human rights bodies and is one of the vivid examples of the use of other international instruments by the ECtHR. In this judgment, the Court considered the opinions of the European Committee of Social Rights, the ILO Committee of Experts and the ILO CFA (*see* paragraphs 20-23 and 26 of this decision) who were unanimous in the definition of essential services and in urging Russia to amend the legislation prohibiting strikes for railway staff. Hopefully, this judgment will make the Government at least (and at last) adopt the list of professions of the railway staff to whom the prohibition of a strike will be addressed. We can hardly expect that the ban will be repealed. It is not surprising that the ECtHR did not require legislative changes as a general measure. According to the new norms of the Federal Constitutional Law 'On the Constitutional Court of the Russian Federation' adopted in 2015, this court has now jurisdiction to decide if it is possible to execute a judgment of ECtHR in light of the provisions of the Russian Constitution. Therefore, taking into account that the position of the Constitutional Court, expressed in 2005, was contrary to the opinion of the ECtHR in the present case, it is very unlikely that any general measure of amending the legislation on the right to strike would be implemented in Russia.

The Court focused on the compatibility of the legislative ban with the Convention generally, and less so on the violation of the particular applicant's rights. This differs significantly from RMT, which stressed that the Court must focus on the effect of the secondary action ban on the applicant in the case. The only point of difference which Ognevenko highlights is that in RMT, the Government had provided information explaining the policy choice of the legislature in favour of a ban, which seems insufficient as a justification for the inconsistencies between the two cases. Ognevenko thus creates further confusion over how cases concerning the right to strike should be analysed and the role which ILO and ESC standards play in that analysis. In any event, as the case law stands at the moment, in particular in light of RMT, it is possible that the right to strike is protected to a lesser extent under Article 11 than ILO and ESC.

This and some further inconsistencies are highlighted in the strongly worded Dissenting Opinion of Judge Dedov in Ognevenko, which starts in an explosive manner: '*The Court imposes certain standards in very controversial circumstances, and what is more important, the standards themselves are not clear because the Court occasionally invents them.*'

He then continues explaining what the problems of the court happen to be: 'In sum, the problems of the Court are of a dual nature: the Court assumes that the domestic authorities could not and/or did not apply the Convention standards because they were prevented from doing so by statutory provisions, even if the domestic courts had in fact struck a balance in order to protect the prevailing public interest within the scope of a legitimate aim. In such a situation (when the rights and freedoms of others are at stake) the Court does not always provide a clear criterion for the proportionality/balancing test.'

From this analysis, a clear pattern seems to stand out: as the Convention is a living instrument, also are the Judges.

This statement is reinforced by two very recent cases that the Court has dealt with on the matter of the right to strike. The year 2021 was indeed one that produced, in the matter of the advancement of the case law, both a key case and a case which could be said to go beyond merely applying the existing case law and some say that it could even be '*one of the most significant cases in European labour law so far this century*'.[413] On the matter of the second case, while what has been written may be true on the matter of balancing of interests and hierarchy of sources, its impact of the right to strike per se is, at best, modest. These are the Barış[414] case and the Holship case.[415]

The first case concerned the dismissal of employees on account of their involvement in a strike organized outside a trade-union context. The Court declared the application inadmissible (incompatible *ratione materiae*), finding that, on the basis of the evidence in the case file, given that the applicants had not been dismissed for having taken part in a demonstration organized by a trade union, or for having asserted professional rights as part of the activities of a trade union, or for having left a specific trade union, or for having decided not to join a specific trade union, they could not effectively claim a right to the freedom of association that was protected under Article 11 of the Convention.

The Court had first to determine the relevant issue, which was not whether individual employees, taking part in unofficial industrial action that was not organized by a trade union, were entitled under national or international law to call or take part in a strike, but rather whether such a right fell within the scope of Article 11.

413. J. Hendy QC, T. Novitz, 'The Holship Case', *Industrial Law Journal* 47:2 (2018): 315-335.
414. Case of Bariş and Others v. Turkey, cited (61).
415. Case of Norwegian Confederation of Trade Unions (LO) and Norwegian Transport Workers' Union (NTF) v. Norway, cited (35).

According to the Court's established case law, strike action is, in principle, protected by Article 11 only in so far as it is initiated by trade-union organizations and considered as being effectively – and not merely presumed to be – part of the trade-union activity. The Court had never accepted that a strike that was not called by a trade union but rather by that trade union's members, or even non-members, was also entitled to the protection of Article 11.[416] In this case, the right to strike was part of the right to organize, but as the action in the present case had not been conducted in the framework of the trade-union organization, it could not be considered that the termination of the applicants' employment contracts had breached their right to strike.

On the basis of the evidence in the case file, it could not effectively be claimed that a right to the freedom of association that was protected under Article 11 was violated. The second case concerned Norway's decision to declare unlawful the announced trade union boycott to pressurize foreign companies into a collective agreement in breach of EEA's freedom of establishment, which was found not in violation of Article 11 of the Convention.

It should be remembered that Norway is a member of the European Free Trade Association (EFTA) and of the EEA, but not a member of the EU. The facts were the following: the applicant trade unions, NTF and LO, entered into a collective framework agreement with the Confederation of Norwegian Enterprise (NHO), the largest employer organization in Norway, and the Norwegian Logistics and Freight Association (NHO logistikk og transport), in respect of a fixed pay scheme for dockworkers at many of Norway's major ports, including the port of Drammen.

Holship Norge AS was not a member of NHO or NHO logistikk og transport and proceeded to employ four persons in the port. NTF then demanded that a collective agreement be entered into and that Holship accept the Framework Agreement. Holship did not agree. The NTF sent a letter with a notice of boycott and successfully sought an advance declaratory judgment that the announced boycott would not be unlawful from the domestic courts. Holship appealed to the Supreme Court, which applied for an advisory opinion by the Court of Justice of the EFTA. The Supreme Court ruled that the boycott would be unlawful.

The Norwegian Supreme Court had recognized that freedom of establishment is a fundamental right in the context of the EEA, so a balance had to be found between this right and those accorded to the plaintiffs under Article 11 of the ECHR, and in the present case, although the announced boycott was intended to protect the interests of the workers, it would have hindered Holship's freedom. Moreover, it is not common ground that the collective action of a boycott enjoys the same protection as a strike.

Repeating the Norwegian Supreme Court's assessments, the ECtHR recalls that while the indirect effect of the boycott announced by the unions would have been to guarantee certain working conditions and pay levels for port workers registered and hired by the Administrative Office, it would still directly have prevented other operators such as Holship from entering that market.

416. Notably, Karaçay v. Turquie, No. 6615/03 (ECtHR, 27 March 2007) and Association of Academics v. Iceland, No. 2451/16 (ECtHR, 15 May 2018).

Furthermore, following the Supreme Court judgment, the relevant social partners had negotiated and concluded a new collective agreement: the restriction of the applicant unions' Article 11 rights had not as such prevented them from engaging in further collective bargaining. Against that background, the Court did not consider that sufficiently 'strong reasons' existed for it to substitute its views for that of the Supreme Court in this case.

Therefore, the Court found that in the particular circumstances of this case, the Supreme Court had advanced relevant and sufficient grounds to justify its final conclusion. What comes to be somehow relevant in this case is what lies beneath the decision of the Court, which we still have to go through and which must not be taken at name value, but be analysed with great care.

Preceding its decision, the Court decided to expose itself further by taking advantage of the case before it to point out that, while it is true that the economic rights and freedoms recognized by the EEA Agreement may sometimes justify restrictions on the rights under Article 11 of the Convention, it is equally true that a collective action, in order to achieve its purpose, may have to interfere with internal market freedoms, such as those at issue in the case examined by the Supreme Court.

The negative economic consequences, which would have resulted from the stoppage of loading and unloading activities resulting from the boycott, would have been an integral part of industrial action, as is the case, for example, in a strike. The implication of this is that the acceding states must ensure that the restrictions imposed on the rights under Article 11 of the Convention do not undermine the essential elements of trade union freedom, without which that freedom would become devoid of substance. Finally, the ECtHR emphasizes that, under the Convention, '*EEA freedom of establishment is not a counterbalancing fundamental right to freedom of association but rather one element, albeit an important one, to be taken into consideration in the assessment of proportionality under Article 11, paragraph 2.*'

It could be said that with this pronouncement, the ECtHR has actually stated that '*the right to strike takes precedence over the "economic freedoms" of the single market*',[417] but we suggest taking a better look at the Court's reasoning and the context. On the matter of the apparent contrast between EEA and ECHR norms, the Court reiterates that it has held that if an organization to which a Contracting State has transferred jurisdiction is considered to protect fundamental rights in a manner which can be considered at least 'equivalent' to that for which the Convention provides, the presumption will be that a State has not departed from the requirements of the Convention when it does no more than implement legal obligations flowing from its membership of the organization.[418]

However, the Court recently[419] stated that the basis for the presumption established by Bosphorus is in principle lacking when it comes to the implementation of EEA

417. As stated by ETUC in its press release following the Judgment, https://www.etuc.org/en/pressrelease/ecthr-ruling-right-strike.
418. This is the Bosphorus presumption of equivalent protection. Bosphorus Hava Yollari Turizm Ve Ticaret Anonim Şirketi v. Ireland No. 45036/98 (ECtHR, 30 June 2005).
419. Konkurrenten.no AS v. Norway No. 47341/15 (ECtHR, 5 November 2019).

law at a domestic level within the framework of the EEA Agreement, due to the specificities of the governing treaties compared to those of the EU. For the purpose of the analysis in that decision, two distinct features were specifically highlighted. First, and in contrast to EU law, there is within the framework of the EEA Agreement itself no direct effect and no supremacy. Second, and although the EFTA Court has expressed the view that the provisions of the EEA Agreement 'are to be interpreted in the light of fundamental rights' in order to enhance coherency between EEA law and EU law, the EEA Agreement does not include the EU Charter of Fundamental Rights or any reference whatsoever to other legal instruments having the same effect. That, of course, is because not all EEA members are EU members also.

The Court proceeds by stating that 'the fact that the EEA agreement does not include the EU Charter is not determinative of the question whether the Bosphorus presumption could apply when it comes to the implementation of EEA law'. However, given one of the other features of EEA law identified by the Court in the Konkurrenten.no decision - the absence of supremacy and direct effect, added to which is the absence of the binding legal effect of advisory opinions from the EFTA Court - and given that the existence of procedural mechanisms for ensuring the protection of substantive fundamental rights guarantees is one of the two conditions for the application of the Bosphorus presumption, the Court leaves it to another case, where questions in relation to the procedural mechanisms under EEA law may arise, to review this issue.

It, therefore, proceeds on the basis that for the purposes of this case, the Bosphorus presumption does not apply to EEA law, then getting to the already-known decision. One thing that must be taken into consideration is the following: EEA agreements non-abundantly counterbalanced by EU treaties and guarantees through directives and regulations embedded in the legal system of the State are not that common. This decision does not really apply to the 'economic freedoms' of the single market, but just to two States: Norway and Iceland.

The brief excursus above shows a clear development in the jurisprudence of the ECtHR on the right to strike in the context of trade union freedom. However, the answer to the question of whether the right to strike is part of the 'essential content' of trade union freedom protected by Article 11 of the Convention cannot currently be found with absolute clarity in the jurisprudence, although, as it has been said, several indications seem to lead the interpreter towards an affirmative solution. At this point, a clarifying intervention by the Grande Chambre of the Court seems desirable. The opportunity could also be used to test the RMT judgment's assertion that 'secondary' actions are entitled to attenuated protection.

It may very well be the case to look at the other side of the Pacific Ocean for inspiration, given the important advance made by the United States–Mexico–Canada Agreement ('USMCA'),[420] which makes the Labour chapter on this matter the most advanced model of the social clause. The clear reference is to the provision, contained

420. The Agreement is a free trade agreement between the Member States. It replaced the North American Free Trade Agreement (NAFTA) implemented in 1994, and it largely maintains or updates the provisions of its predecessor.

in a note to the text, that '*the right to strike is linked to the right to freedom of association, which cannot be realized without protecting the right to strike*'.[421] This recognition of the right to strike and its protection through the social clause was by no means taken for granted and sounds like an absolute novelty in the history of international trade treaties.[422] Considering the long-standing internal dispute within the ILO on the interpretation of Convention No. 87,[423] the importance of this statement, which surprisingly also interests the European front in view of the different axiological orientations expressed on the matter by the ECtHR[424] and the Court of Justice of the EU,[425] can be very well understood.

And it could be taken as a reference.

421. Article 23.3 USMCA, note No. 5.
422. L. Compa, 'Trump, Trade, and Trabajo: Renegotiating Nafta's Labor Accord in a Fraught Political Climate', *Indiana Journal of Global Legal Studies*. 26:1, Article 8 (2019), p. 263.
423. Which pitted the Committee of Independent Experts and the CFA, on the one hand, and the employer component of the ILO, on the other, until the agreement reached in 2015.
424. G. Raimondi, *Il diritto di sciopero è elemento essenziale della libertà di associazione? Evoluzione della giurisprudenza della Corte europea dei diritti dell'uomo, in* Lavoro, Diritti, Europa 2019 / 1, p. 61.
425. V. De Stefano, 'La protezione del diritto di sciopero nella dialettica tra corti e organi di supervisione internazionali', *Giorn. dir. lav. rel. ind.* 134:3 (2014): 461.

Conclusions

In this book, we have considered more than fifty cases relevant to labour law, including issues of individual and collective labour law and the realization of such human rights as the freedom of religion and expression, or the right to privacy at the workplace. We have taken a period of five years which might be rather illustrative provided the huge challenge to workers' rights and human rights in the COVID era and the post-COVID economic hardships.

We pursued two key objectives: to establish certain trends in the jurisprudence of the ECtHR in this period and to demonstrate the applicability of ECHR for the protection of labour rights and human rights. Summing up the determined trends, the following key findings should be outlined.

Determining the scope of labour-related rights of the ECHR, the Court largely relies on the ILO standards, the positions of the ILO bodies (CFA, CEACR), and the ESC. This is not a new trend; throughout its history, the Court referred to these instruments to legitimise the interpretation of the Convention. However, a new point might be found in broadening the interpretation of forced labour in line with the changes brought to the ILO Forced Labour Convention No. 29 by Protocol No. 29 adopted in 2014. This protocol provides obligations of the states to ensure the prevention of forced labour including human trafficking, identification and protection of victims as well as the remedy for the damage suffered. The Court's recent case law under Article 4 of the ECHR (forced labour) considered the problem of human trafficking, strengthens the states' obligation to identify victims, and encourages the members of the CoE to ensure that there is an opportunity for a 'non-punishment approach' to the offences committed by the victims of human trafficking. However, in line with the previous case law, the Court does not consider under this article the cases when the applicants had to perform additional work without being paid.

Struggling with discrimination, the Court, relying on the broad interpretation of Article 8 (respect to private life which is read as including the right to establish and develop relations of professional nature), granted protection against gender discrimination in access to employment (*see* Demirel v. Turkey). Also, it was open to considering the cases of discrimination on grounds not explicitly listed in Article 14 (*see* Saumier v. France).

The most vivid results of the ECtHR's protection of workers might be found in the recent jurisprudence under Article 8. The Court adopted a very elaborate framework for the consideration of employees' privacy protection cases (*see* Bărbulescu v. Romania). Having stated that unfair dismissal might violate the right to respect for private life, it opened the door for numerous cases, making ECtHR almost a pan-European last-instance employment tribunal. In Denisov v. Ukraine, the ECtHR provided a very detailed explanation of the criteria which should be evaluated if the application concerns unfair dismissal.

Applying Article 9 (freedom of religion), the Court considered cases on the right of contentious objection to military service and elaborated certain quality requirements to the regulation of alternative service to be considered complying with the norms of the ECHR and listed the factors which are relevant for the establishment of the nature and character of the alternative service (Adyan and Others v. Armenia). These contributions might be very important for the countries of the Council of Europe where there is still compulsory military service.

Evaluating the recent contributions to the protection of employees' freedom of expression, we have noted the growing number of cases connected with the expression of opinions in social media. Considering these cases, the Court recognized that workplace-related free speech does not only protect comments that demonstrably contribute to a debate on a public matter but also covers topics of purely professional interest if it does not adversely affect the business interests of an employer (*see* Herbai v. Hungary). Also, it introduced a framework for considering cases where employees who expressed an opinion on the social network through 'likes' were dismissed or somehow penalized; the list of questions to be answered by the national courts might be found in the Melike v. Turkey case. The recent cases considered under Article 10 (the freedom of expression) demonstrate the current threat to the independence of national judges in some countries of the CoE. Considering these applications, the ECtHR underlined the need to take into account the 'chilling effect' that disciplinary measures imposed for the expression of a certain opinion might have on public servants. Therefore, a proportionality between the interference against freedom of expression and the legitimate aim pursued must be ensured (*see* Goryaynova v. Ukraine, Todorova v. Bulgaria, Kövesi v. Romania).

Finally, considering the cases on the protection of collective labour rights, we have established that the ECtHR broadly interprets Article 11. However, the recent case law reveals certain points of divergence and conflict between the ECHR and ILO and ESC guarantees.

The second objective of the research consisted in demonstrating the applicability of ECHR for the protection of labour rights and human rights both at the level of the Council of Europe and the national one. The mentioned generous approach of the ECtHR to consider unfair dismissal as a violation of the right to respect for private life is one of the vivid signs of such applicability. These cases should increase the attention of European labour lawyers to the ECtHR. We can evidence the growing number of cases about the violations of the positive obligations of states in respect of private sector employees thus broadening the scope of application of the ECHR. Also, we have determined that some landmark cases are referred to in the case law of national courts at different levels of the judicial system, including also the constitutional courts. Our research demonstrates that many legal positions of the ECtHR might be very valuable for adjudication of employment disputes at the national level, and we believe that it is important to include relevant information about these positions in all the textbooks on national labour law in the countries of the Council of Europe.

Annex

ECtHR, DENISOV v. UKRAINE (76639/11) GC 25/09/2018, Paras 102-117:

102. In the cases falling into the above-mentioned category, the Court applies the concept of 'private life' on the basis of two different approaches: (α) identification of the 'private life' issue as the reason for the dispute (reason-based approach) and (β) deriving the 'private life' issue from the consequences of the impugned measure (consequence-based approach).

(α) Reason-based approach

103. Complaints concerning the exercise of professional functions have been found to fall within the ambit of 'private life' when factors relating to private life were regarded as qualifying criteria for the function in question and when the impugned measure was based on reasons encroaching upon the individual's freedom of choice in the sphere of private life.

104. Thus, in the area of public service, where measures taken by State authorities were contested, the Court has found, for example, that investigations by the military police into the applicants' homosexuality and their consequent administrative discharge on the sole ground of their sexual orientation directly interfered with their right to respect for private life (*see Smith and Grady*, cited above, § 71). In *Özpınar* (cited above), proceedings for the applicant's dismissal as a judge fell under Article 8 of the Convention because they concerned not only her professional performance but also targeted aspects of her private life, in particular her close private relationships, the clothes and make-up she wore and the fact that she lived separately from her mother (*ibid.*, §§ 43 and 47). In another case the applicant's transfer to a less important post within the public service raised an issue under 'private life' given that such a measure amounted to a disguised penalty and had been prompted by reasons relating to the applicant's beliefs and his wife's clothing (*see Sodan*, cited above, §§ 47-49).

105. The Court has applied similar logic from the standpoint of the positive obligations to carry out a careful balancing exercise between the private interests of employees and those of a non-governmental employer when the reasons for the dismissal related directly to the applicants' conduct in their private life, such as an extramarital relationship (*see Obst*, cited above, §§ 43 et seq.) or living with a new partner after separation (*see Schüth*, cited above, §§ 57 et seq.). Where a private company dismissed an employee on the basis of monitoring of his correspondence by his employer in the workplace, such a measure fell within the ambit of Article 8 in so far as it concerned the 'correspondence' and because it encroached upon the reasonable possibility of enjoying any 'private life' in the workplace (*see Bărbulescu*, cited above, §§ 81 and 127).

106. As can be seen from these examples, the underlying reasons for the impugned measure affecting professional life may be linked to the individual's private life and these reasons themselves may render Article 8 applicable.

(β) Consequence-based approach

107. When the reasons for imposing a measure affecting an individual's professional life are not linked to the individual's private life, an issue under Article 8 may still arise in so far as the impugned measure has or may have serious negative effects on the individual's private life. In this connection the Court has taken into account negative consequences as regards (i) impact on the individual's 'inner circle', in particular where there are serious material consequences, (ii) the individual's opportunities 'to establish and develop relationships with others', and (iii) the impact on the individual's reputation.

108. On the basis of that approach, the Court has found that the dismissal of a judge on the grounds of a violation of his professional duties amounting to a breach of the judicial oath affected a wide range of his professional and other relationships. The dismissal also had a negative impact on the applicant's 'inner circle' in view of his loss of earnings, and it also affected his reputation (*see Oleksandr Volkov*, cited above, § 166). The refusal to allow an applicant who was a foreigner to sit for the Bar examinations in Greece fell within the scope of Article 8 because it affected her personal choice as to the way she wished to pursue her professional and private life (*see Bigaeva*, cited above, §§ 24 and 25). The entry of an applicant's name in the bankruptcy register entailed a series of legal restrictions on the exercise of her professional activities and civil rights. It therefore affected the applicant's opportunities to develop relationships with the outside world and fell within the sphere of her private life (*see Campagnano*, cited above, § 54). A far-reaching ban on taking up private-sector employment has also been found to affect 'private life' (*see Sidabras and Džiautas*, cited above, § 47).

109. Where no reason-based approach justifies the applicability of Article 8, an analysis of the effects of the impugned measure on the above-mentioned aspects of private life is necessary to conclude that the complaint falls within the scope of 'private life'. Nevertheless, this division does not preclude cases in which the Court may find it appropriate to employ both approaches in combination, examining whether there is a private life issue in the underpinning reasons for the impugned measure and, in addition, analysing the consequences of the measure (*see Fernández Martínez*, cited above, §§ 110-12).

(iv) Minimum level of severity of the alleged violation

In this connection the Court has taken into account negative consequences as regards (i) impact on the individual's 'inner circle', in particular where there are serious material consequences, (ii) the individual's opportunities 'to establish and develop relationships with others', and (iii) the impact on the individual's reputation.

110. In cases where the Court employs the consequence-based approach, the analysis of the seriousness of the impugned measure's effects occupies an important place. The Court has addressed the issue of the seriousness or severity of the alleged violation in several contexts. Notably, it has done so when assessing the 'significant disadvantage' under Article 35 § 3 (b) of the Convention as an explicit admissibility requirement for the whole system of the Convention rights (see, for example, *Giusti v. Italy*, no. 13175/03, § 34, 18 October 2011; *Gagliano Giorgi v. Italy*, no. 23563/07, § 56, ECHR 2012 (extracts); and *El Kaada v. Germany*, no. 2130/10, § 41, 12 November 2015). The Court has also consistently applied a threshold of severity in cases concerning Article 3 of the Convention (see, for example, *Jalloh v. Germany* [GC], no. 54810/00, § 67, ECHR 2006-IX; *Gäfgen v. Germany* [GC], no. 22978/05, § 88, ECHR 2010; and *Bouyid v. Belgium* [GC], no. 23380/09, § 86, ECHR 2015).

111. The concept of threshold of severity has been specifically examined under Article 8. In environmental cases, in particular, an arguable claim under Article 8 may arise where an environmental hazard attains a level of severity resulting in significant impairment of the applicant's ability to enjoy his or her home or private or family life. The Court has ruled that the assessment of this minimum level in such cases is relative and depends on all the circumstances of the case, such as the intensity and duration of the nuisance and its physical or mental effects on the individual's health or quality of life (*see Fadeyeva v. Russia*, no. 55723/00, §§ 68 and 69, ECHR 2005-I-V-; *Dubetska and Others v. Ukraine*, no. 30499/03, § 105, 10 February 2011; and Grimkovskaya v. Ukraine, no. 38182/03, § 58, 21 July 2011). This approach has also been applied in nuisance cases under Article 8 with close similarities to the environmental cases mentioned above (*see Borysiewicz v. Poland*,

no. 71146/01, § 51, 1 July 2008, and *Udovičić v. Croatia*, no. 27310/09, § 137, 24 April 2014).

112. In addition, the Court has ruled that an attack on a person's reputation must attain a certain level of seriousness and be made in a manner causing prejudice to personal enjoyment of the right to respect for private life (*see A. v. Norway*, no. 28070/06, §§ 63-64, 9 April 2009; *Polanco Torres and Movilla Polanco v. Spain*, no. 34147/06, §§ 40 and 44, 21 September 2010; *Axel Springer AG*, cited above, § 83; *Delfi AS v. Estonia* [GC], no. 64569/09, § 137, ECHR 2015; and *Bédat v. Switzerland* [GC], no. 56925/08, § 72, ECHR 2016). This requirement covers social reputation in general as well as professional reputation in particular (for the latter, *see Medžlis Islamske Zajednice Brčko and Others v. Bosnia and Herzegovina* [GC], nos. 17224/11, §§ 76 and 105-06, ECHR 2017).

113. In the recent case of Erményi the Court found that the applicant's dismissal from the administrative position of Vice-President of the Supreme Court constituted an interference with his right to respect for private life (*see* Erményi, cited above, § 31). Even though the Court did not elaborate on this point, in the absence of the parties' submissions in that regard, it implied that the impugned measure had seriously affected the applicant's private life. That finding cannot be read as presuming that the applicant's dismissal had 'automatically' generated an issue in the sphere of private life. In that regard the Court reiterates that the threshold of severity occupies an important place in cases where the existence of a private-life issue is examined according to the consequence-based approach.

114. It is thus an intrinsic feature of the consequence-based approach within Article 8 that convincing evidence showing that the threshold of severity was attained has to be submitted by the applicant. As the Grand Chamber has held, applicants are obliged to identify and explain the concrete repercussions on their private life and the nature and extent of their suffering, and to substantiate such allegations in a proper way (*see Gillberg*, cited above, §§ 70-73). According to the requirement of exhaustion of domestic remedies, such allegations have to be sufficiently raised at the domestic level.

(v) Conclusions: the scope of Article 8 in employment-related disputes

115. The Court concludes from the above case-law that employment-related disputes are not *per se* excluded from the scope of 'private life' within the meaning of Article 8 of the Convention. There are some typical aspects of private life which may be affected in such disputes by dismissal, demotion, non-admission to a profession or other similarly unfavourable measures. These aspects include (i) the applicant's 'inner circle', (ii) the applicant's opportunity to establish and develop relationships with others, and (iii) the applicant's social and professional reputation. There are two ways in which a private-life issue would usually arise in such a dispute: either because of

the underlying reasons for the impugned measure (in that event the Court employs the reason-based approach) or – in certain cases – because of the consequences for private life (in that event the Court employs the consequence-based approach).

116. If the consequence-based approach is at stake, the threshold of severity with respect to all the above-mentioned aspects assumes crucial importance. It is for the applicant to show convincingly that the threshold was attained in his or her case. The applicant has to present evidence substantiating consequences of the impugned measure. The Court will only accept that Article 8 is applicable where these consequences are very serious and affect his or her private life to a very significant degree.

117. The Court has established criteria for assessing the severity or seriousness of alleged violations in different regulatory contexts. An applicant's suffering is to be assessed by comparing his or her life before and after the measure in question. The Court further considers that in determining the seriousness of the consequences in employment-related cases it is appropriate to assess the subjective perceptions claimed by the applicant against the background of the objective circumstances existing in the particular case. This analysis would have to cover both the material and the non-material impact of the alleged measure. However, it remains for the applicant to define and substantiate the nature and extent of his or her suffering, which should have a causal connection with the impugned measure. Having regard to the rule of exhaustion of domestic remedies, the essential elements of such allegations must be sufficiently raised before the domestic authorities dealing with the matter.

Bibliography

Aisling R. *The Prohibition of Torture: A Guide to the Implementation of Article 3 of the European Convention on Human Rights*. Handbook No. 6 2003.

Alessandra Di M. 'National Constitutions and the ECHR', in: Giorgio Repetto (ed.) *The Constitutional Relevance of the ECHR in Domestic and European Law. An Italian Perspective*. Intersentia Cambridge, Portland, 2013, 133.

Alexandra T. Of Firearms and Weak Women: Sex Discrimination in Hülya Ebru Demirel v. Turkey, 31 July 2018, https://strasbourgobservers.com/2018/07/31/of-firearms-and-weak-women-sex-discrimination-in-hulya-ebru-demirel-v-turkey/.

Alicia H. Gruba and Others V. Russia: The ECtHR Repeats Its Konstantin Markin V. Russia Jurisprudence But (Again) Misses a Child-Oriented Perspective. 1 October 2021. https://strasbourgobservers.com/2021/10/01/gruba-and-others-v-russia-the-ecthr-repeats-its-konstantin-markin-v-russia-jurisprudence-but-again-misses-a-child-oriented-perspective/.

Andrew H. 'Neutrality and Workplace Restrictions on Headscarves and Religious Dress: Lessons from Achbita and Bougnaoui'. *Industrial Law Journal* 47:1 (2018): 149-164.

Atkinson, J. 'Workplace Monitoring and the Right to Private Life at Work'. *Modern Law Review* 81:4 (2018): 688-700.

Bates, E. *The Evolution of the European Convention on Human Rights: From Its Inception to the Creation of a Permanent Court of Human Rights*. Oxford University Press 2010, 59.

Niklas, B., Lörcher K., Schömann I., and Clauwaert S., eds, *The European Social Charter and the Employment Relation*. Hart Publishing 2017.

Stylogiannis C. 'The Protection of the Right to Strike under the European Convention on Human Rights'. *UCL Journal of Law and Jurisprudence* 6 (2017): 142.

Calin D. The Recent ECtHR Judgment Kövesi v. Romania: Reactions of Romanian Authorities and Implications Regarding the Rule of Law (8 January 2022). Strasbourg Observers, 16 June 2020, https://strasbourgobservers.com/2020/06

/16/the-recent-ecthr-judgment-kovesi-v-romania-reactions-of-romanian-authorities-and-implications-regarding-the-rule-of-law/.

Carmona Bayona E. 'Libertad religiosa y relaciones laborales. Estudios de las sentencias más emblemáticas del Tribunal Europeo de Derechos Humanos y del Tribunal Constitucional Español.' *Derecho global. Estudios sobre derecho y justicia* 6:16 (2020): 239-250.

Chrun E. 'Help Me Help You: How the EU Made Romania's Anticorruption Reforms a (Temporary) Success'. *East European Politics* (2022): 1-21.

Collected Edition of the 'Travaux Préparatoires' of the European ECHR on Human Rights: Preparatory Commission of the Council of Europe, Committee of Ministers, Consultative Assembly, 11 May-8 September 1949. Council of Europe. BRILL, 1975, p. 116.

Curtis K. '100 Years of the ILO in Action: Reflections on Inclusive Collective Representation and the Organization's Quest for Social Justice', *King's Law Journal* 32:2 (2021): 184.

Mccann D. and Fudge J. 'Unacceptable Forms of Work: A Multidimensional Model'. *International Labour Review* 156:2 (2017): 147-184.

Data Protection and Privacy, Enforcing Rights in a Changing World, Bloomsbury Publishing (2021): 73.

Davies A.C.L., 'One Step Forward, Two Steps Back? The Viking and Laval Cases in the ECJ'. *Industrial Law Journal* 37:2 (2008): 126-148.

Dorssemont F., Lörcher K. *The European Convention on Human Rights and the Employment Relation*. Oxford Hart Publishing, 2013.

Dukes R. 'Constitutionalizing Employment Relations: Sinzheimer, Kahn-Freund, and the Role of Labour Law'. *Journal of Law and Society* 35:3 (2008): 341-363.

Ebert F. & Oelz V. *Bridging the Gap Between Labour Rights and Human Rights: The Role of ILO Law in Regional Human Rights Courts*. ILO, 2012.

ECtHR, Guide on Article 8 of the Convention: Right to Respect for Private and Family Life. Updated on 31 August 2022.

Sychenko E. 'Individual Labour Rights as Human Rights: The Contributions of the European Court of Human Rights to Worker's Rights Protection'. Roger Blanpain, Frank Hendrickx (eds). *Wolters Kluwer International. Bulletin of Comparative Labour Relations*, Vol. 96. 2017, 268 p.

Elliott J. *The Role of Consent in Human Trafficking*. Routledge, New York, 2014.

European Bureau for Conscientious Objection. Annual Report Conscientious Objection to Military Service in Europe 2021. https://www.ohchr.org/sites/default/files/2022-05/EBCO-HRC50.pdf.

European Commission of Human Rights. Preparatory works on Article 3 of the ECHR. 22.05.1956. Available at: https://www.echr.coe.int/LibraryDocs/Travaux/ECHRTravaux-ART3-DH(56)5-EN1674940.pdf.

Dorssemont, F. 'How the European Court of Human Rights Gave Us Enerji to Cope with Laval and Viking', in: Marie-Ange Moraeu (ed.), *Before and after the Economic Crisis: What Implications for the 'European Social Model'*, Edward Elgar Publishing Limited, 2014, 217 & 220.

Federation of Offshore Workers' Trade Unions and Others v. Norway No. 38190/97 (ECtHR, 27 June 2002).

Fudge J. 'Constitutionalizing Labour Rights in Europe', in: T. Campbell, K. Ewing & A. Tompkins (eds) *The Legal Protection of Human Rights: Sceptical Essays*, Oxford: Oxford University Press, 2011, 244-267.

Rodgers G., Lee E., Swepston L. and Van Daele J. 'The International Labour Organization and the Quest for Social Justice'. *International Labour Office* Geneva (2009): 1919-2009.

Vettori G. Diritti fondamentali e diritti sociali. Una riflessione fra due crisi, in Eur. dir. priv., n. 3, 2011.

Gagne D., and Dupuis M-J. 'Constitutionnalisation du Droit du Travail et Transformation du Devoir de Representation S indicale: Quelques Questionnements Concernant les Clauses Orphelin'. *Canadian Lab. & Emp. LJ* 20 (2017): 1.

Gerasimova E. & Kolganova S. 'The Right for Strike in ILO Jurisprudence: Crisis of Recognition?' *Law Journal of the Higher School of Economics* 4 (2016): 184-97.

Gernigon B., Odero A., & Guido H. 'ILO Principles Concerning the Right to Strike'. *International Labour Review* 137:4 (1998) https://www.ilo.org/wcmsp5/groups/public/---ed_norm/---normes/documents/publication/wcms_087987.pdf.

Clayton G. 'Asylum Seekers in Europe: MSS v. Belgium and Greece', *Human Rights Law Review* 11:4 (2011): 758-773.

Guide on Article 6 of the European Convention on Human Rights Right to a fair trial (civil limb) Updated to 30 April 2022, https://www.echr.coe.int/documents/guide_art_6_eng.pdf.

Harris D., O'Boyle M., Warbrick C., *Law of the European Convention on Human Rights*. 2nd edn. Oxford University Press 2009, 108.

Hill H. '"Eweida v. United Kingdom": The Right to Manifest Religion under Article 9 of the ECHR'. *European Human Rights Law Review* 2 (2013): 187-193.

Hornung-Draus R. 'The Right to Strike in the ILO System of Standards: Facts and Fiction'. *Comparative Labour Law and Policy Journal* 39:3 (2018): 531-536.

Collins H. 'An Emerging Human Right to Protection against Unjustified Dismissal', *Industrial Law Journal* 50:1 (2021): 36-69, https://doi.org/10.1093/indlaw/dwaa003.

Hughes K. 'Human Trafficking, SM v. Croatia and the Conceptual Evolution of Article 4 ECHR'. *The Modern Law Review* 85:4 (2022): 1044-1061.

Hungler S. 'Compulsory Vaccination and Fundamental Human Rights in the World of Work' *Studia Iuridica Lublinensia* 31:1 (2022): 63-77.

Hendy QC J., Novitz T. 'The Holship Case', *Industrial Law Journal* 47:2 (2018): 315-335.

Judge Matscher F. 'Methods of Interpretation of the Convention', in: R.St. J. Macdonald et al. (ed.) *The European System for the Protection of Human Rights*, Martinus Nijhoff Publishers, Leiden, 1993, 69-70.

Arabadjieva K. *A Framework for Interpreting the Right to Freedom of Association of Workers and Trade Unions in European Human Rights Law*, PhD Thesis. University of Oxford, 2019.

Ewing K.D., Hendy QC J. 'The Dramatic Implications of Demir and Baykara'. *Industrial Law Journal* 39 (2010): 41.

Ewing K. 'United Kingdom', in: C. LA Macchia (ed.), *The Right to Strike in the EU, The Complexity of the Norms and Safeguarding Efficacy*, Ediesse, Rome, 2011.

Kane, Gillian. 'Building a House upon Sand? Human Trafficking, Forced Labor, and Exploitation of Prostitution in SM v. Croatia'. *International Labour Rights Case Law* 7:1 (2021): 74-79.

Karaçay v. Turquie, No 6615/03 (ECtHR, 27 March 2007).

Konkurrenten.no AS v. Norway No. 47341/15 (ECtHR, 5 November 2019).

Krasser A. 'Compulsory Vaccination in a Fundamental Rights Perspective: Lessons from the ECtHR'. *ICL Journal* 15:2 (2021) 207-233. https://doi.org/10.1515/icl-2021-0010.

Compa L. 'Trump, Trade, and Trabajo: Renegotiating NAFTA's Labor Accord in a Fraught Political Climate'. *Indiana Journal of Global Legal Studies*, 26:8 Article 8(2019): 263.

Letsas G. 'The ECHR as a Living Instrument: Its Meaning and Its Legitimacy' (14 March 2012). Available at SSRN: http://ssrn.com/abstract=2021836.

Likić-Brborić B. and Schierup C-U. 'Labour Rights as Human Rights? Trajectories in the Global Governance of Migration'. *Migration, Precarity, & Global Governance: Challenges and Opportunities for Labour* (2015): 223-244.

Lucifora A. 'From Old Slavery to New Forms of Exploitation: A Reflection on the Conditions of Irregular Migrant Labour After the Chowdury Case'. *New Journal of European Criminal Law* 10:3 (2019): 251-267.

Forde M. 'The European Convention on Human Rights and Labor Law'. *The American Journal of Comparative Law* 31 (1983) 301-332. For an excursus on the most relevant jurisprudence, *see also* Raimondi G. Il diritto di sciopero è elemento essenziale della libertà di associazione? Evoluzione della giurisprudenza della Corte europea dei diritti dell'uomo, in Lavoro, Diritti, Europa 2019 / 1.

Maher J. 'Eweida and Others: A New Era for Article 9?'. *International & Comparative Law Quarterly* 63:1 (2014): 213-233.

Mahoney P. 'The European Convention on Royal Rights: Royalty, Aristocracy and the European Convention on Human Rights' in: La Promotion de la Justice, *Des Droits de L'homme Et Du Règlement Des Conflits Par Le Droit International edited by Marcelo Gustavo Kohen*. Martinus Nijhoff Publishers, Leiden, 2007. 341.

Maioni C. 'I simboli religiosi nella giurisprudenza europea tra libertà religiosa e libertà di impresa (Religious Symbols in European Case Law: Limits to Religious Freedom in Workplace).' *University of Milano-Bicocca School of Law Research Paper* 18:8 (2018).

Mangan D. 'Does an online professional profile violate an employer's confidentiality?'. *European Labour Law Journal* 12:1 (2021): 102-104.

Manole and 'Romanian Farmers Direct' v. Romania No. 46551/06 (ECtHR, 16 June 2015).

Mantouvalou V., 'Labour Rights in the European Convention on Human Rights: An Intellectual Justification for an Integrated Approach to Interpretation'. *Human Rights Law Review* 13:3 (2013): 529-555.

Mantouvalou, V. 'Human Rights and Unfair Dismissal: Private Acts in Public Spaces'. *Modern Law Review* 71:6 (2008): 939.

Mantouvalou V. 'Labour Rights in the European Convention on Human Rights: An Intellectual Justification for an Integrated Approach to Interpretation'. H*uman Rights Law Review* 13:3 (2013): 529-555.

Merrills J., *The Development of International Law by the European Court of Human Rights*. Manchester University Press, 1988.

Hashemi M. 2019/29: Eweida versus Achbita: A Storm in a Teacup (EU), *European Employment Law* Cases 174 (2019).

Napoletano N., 'Estensione e limiti della dimensione economica e sociale della Convenzione europea dei diritti umani in tempi di crisi finanziaria', in *Diritti umani e diritto internazionale*, 2:8 (2014).

O'Cinneíde C. 'The European Social Charter and EU Labour Law'. *Research Handbook on EU Labour Law*. Edward Elgar Publishing, 2016. 191-214.

Olsen C.B. 'When Mandatory Exercise at Work Meets Employees' Rights to Privacy and Non-discrimination: A Comparative and European Perspective'. *European Labour Law Journal* 12:3 (2021): 338-362.

Collins P.M. *Putting Human Rights to Work: Labour Law, the ECHR, and the Employment Relation*, Oxford University Press, 2022.

Pati R. 'States' Positive Obligations with Respect to Human Trafficking: ECtHR Breaks New Ground in Rantsev v. Cyprus & Russia'. *Boston University International Law Journal* 29:1 (2011): 141.

Pearson M. 'Article 9 at a Crossroads: Interference Before and after Eweida'. *Human Rights Law Review* 13:3 (2013): 580-602.

Pellonpaa M. 'Continuity and Change in the Case-Law of the European Court of Human Rights' in: La Promotion de la Justice, *Des Droits de L'homme Et Du Règlement Des Conflits Par Le Droit International edited by Marcelo Gustavo Kohen*. Martinus Nijhoff Publishers, 2007. 409.

Perulli A., Brino V. *Handbook of International Labour Law, e-Book*, Giappichelli Editore, 2018.

Piotrowicz R. and Sorrentino L. 'The Non-punishment Provision with Regard to Victims of Trafficking: A Human Rights Approach 1'. *Routledge Handbook of Human Trafficking*. Routledge, 2017. 171-184.

Preparatory work on Article 4 of the Convention. Council of Europe. 1962. 3, Available at: http://www.echr.coe.int/LibraryDocs/Travaux/ECHRTravaux-ART4-DH(62)10-BIL1712017.PDF (accessed 1 February 2015).

Professions Prohibited to Women: Gender Discrimination Human Rights Report of the ADC 'Memorial'. March 2018. Available at: https://adcmemorial.org/wp-content/uploads/forbidden_2018RUwww.pdf (accessed 20 December 2022).

Rijken C. 'When Bad Labour Conditions Become Exploitation', in: Conny Rijken and Tesseltje de Lange (eds) *Towards a Decent Labour Market for Low-Waged Migrant Workers*. Amsterdam University Press B.V., Amsterdam, 2018: 189-206.

Bartole. S, DE SENA P., ZAGREBELSKY V. *Commentario breve alla CEDU*, Cedam, 2012.

Emploi A. S., Institutions et technologie: Quelques problèmes de politique générale, Revue international de travail. 135:3-4 (1996): 488.

Riggins S. 'Limitations of the Right to Manifest Religion in European Private Companies: Achbita v. G4S Secure Solutions NV under Article 9 of the ECHR and Article 18 of the ICCPR', *American University International Law Review* 33:4 (2018): 977-1018.

Shim M. 'Restrictions on Alternative Service and Conscientious Objection: Focusing on the Jurisprudence of the European Court of Human Rights'. *European Constitutional Studies* 31 (2019): 243-280. In Korean.

Nouwt S. and de Vries B.R. 'Introduction', in: Sjaak Nouwt, Berend R. de Vries, Corien Prins, (eds) *Reasonable Expectations of Privacy? Eleven Country Reports on Camera Surveillance and Workplace Privacy*. T.M.C. Asser Press. The Hague, 2005, p. 3.

Vladislava S.J. and others v. Austria and the strengthening of states' obligation to identify victims of human trafficking, 7 February 2017: https://strasbourgobservers.com/2017/02/07/j-and-others-v-austria-and-the-strengthening-of-states-obligation-to-identify-victims-of-human-trafficking/.

Swepston L., 'Crisis in the ILO Supervisory System: Dispute Over the Right to Strike', *International Journal of Comparative Labour Law and Industrial Relations*, 2, 2013, 199-218.

Sychenko E. Gracheva V., and Rodichev M. 'Modern Slavery in Russia: Exploitation Without Chains'. *Italian Labour Law e-Journal* 14:1 (2021): 261-274.

Sychenko E. 'ILO Contributions to the Jurisprudence of International Human Rights Bodies'. *Zbornik Pravnog fakulteta u Zagrebu* 71:6 (2021): 897-920.

Novitz T. *International and European Protection of the Right to Strike: A Comparative Study of Standards Set by the International Labour Organization, the Council of Europe and the European Union*. Oxford University Press 2013, 180.

Mortier T., Todorova V. M. Bulgaria: Bulgaria Joins List of Serious Rule of Law Offenders, 8 December 2021. https://strasbourgobservers.com/2021/12/08/miroslava-todorova-v-bulgaria-bulgaria-joins-list-of-serious-rule-of-law-offenders/.

Campbell T., Ewing K. and Tompkins A., eds, Oxford: Oxford University Press, 2011, Available at SSRN: https://ssrn.com/abstract=1551587.

Françoise T. *The European Convention on Human Rights and the Economic Crisis: The Issue of Poverty*. EUI Working papers, AEL 2013/8.

Teklè T. 'The Contribution of the ILO's International Labour Standards System to the European Court of Human Rights' Jurisprudence in the Field of Non-discrimination', *Industrial Law Journal*, 49:1 (2020): 86-112.

De Stefano V., La protezione del diritto di sciopero nella dialettica tra corti e or-gani di supervisione internazionali, in Giorn. dir. lav. rel. ind., 2014, 134, 3.

Ebert V. F., Oelz M. Bridging the Gap Between Labour Rights and Human Rights: The Role of ILO Law in Regional Human Rights Courts, IILS Discussion paper DP/2/212/2012, ILO, Geneve, 2012.

van der Sloot B. 'Expectations of Privacy: The Three Tests Deployed by the European Court of Human Rights'. in: Dara Hallinan, Ronald Leenes, Paul De Hert (eds).

Data Protection and Privacy Enforcing Rights in a Changing World. Hart Publishing 2022: 67-96.

van der Stegen B. La liberté religieuse dans la vie professionnelle: du neuf depuis l'arrêt Eweida et autres c. Royaume-Uni?. Faculté de droit et de criminologie, Université catholique de Louvain, 2016. Prom: Dorssemont, Filip. http://hdl.handle.net/2078.1/thesis:7280.

Verstraete, A. G., & Pierce, A. 'Workplace drug testing in Europe', *Forensic Science International* 121:1 (2001): 114.

Vickers L. 'Achbita and Bougnaoui: One Step Forward and Two Steps Back for Religious Diversity in the Workplace'. *European Labour Law Journal* 8 (2017): 232-257.

Vickers L. 'Freedom of Religion or Belief and Employment Law'. *Religion & Human Rights* 12:2-3 (2017): 165.

Villiger M.E. 'Prohibition of Discrimination (Article 14 of the Convention)'. *Handbook on the European Convention on Human Rights*. Brill Nijhoff, 2022, pp. 580-591.

Stoyanova V. The Grand Chamber Judgment in S.M. v. Croatia: Human Trafficking, Prostitution and the Definitional Scope of Article 4 ECHR. 3 July 2020. Available at: https://strasbourgobservers.com/2020/07/03/the-grand-chamber-judgment-in-s-m-v-croatia-human-trafficking-prostitution-and-the-definitional-scope-of-article-4-echr/ (accessed 20 June 2021).

Yanini M.M. 'Libertad de crítica de la persona trabajadora como derecho de alerta: de la lucha contra la corrupción a la protección medioambiental: Comentario a la Sentencia del Tribunal Europeo de Derechos Humanos de 8 de octubre de 2020 (Goryaynova v. Ukraine).' *Revista de Trabajo y Seguridad Social. CEF*, 453, (2020): 207-215.

Yiannaros A. 'The Criminalisation of Conscientious Objection to Military Service in Turkey and Azerbaijan: Time for Action?'. *International Journal of Human Rights and Constitutional Studies* 8:3 (2021): 197-217.

Valery Z. 'Problems of Implementation of the Human Rights Convention' *Journal of Foreign Law and Comparative Law* 5:54 (2015): 812-819. doi:10.12737/16128.

Zorkin, V., The Limits of Pliability (Predel ustupchivosti) Rossyskaya gazeta, 29 October 2010.

Table of Cases

BCLR - BULLETIN OF COMPARATIVE LABOUR RELATIONS

Vol. Author/Title/Year/ISBN

1. Roger Blanpain, *Individual Employment Contracts: Collective Agreements,* 1970.
2. Roger Blanpain, *Social Planning,* 1971 (ISBN 90-312-0018-2).
3. Roger Blanpain, *Guaranteed Income Funds,* 1972 (ISBN 90-312-0019-0).
4. Roger Blanpain, *Employee Participation at the Level of the Enterprise,* 1973 (ISBN 90-312-0020-4).
5. Roger Blanpain, *Vastheid van Betrekking: Staking en Bezetting,* 1974.
6. Roger Blanpain, *Labour Law and Industrial Relations (International Bibliography),* 1975 (ISBN 90-312-0023-9).
7. Roger Blanpain, *Multinational Enterprises,* 1976 (ISBN 90-312-0024-7).
8. Roger Blanpain, *Worker's Participation in the European Company,* 1977 (ISBN 90-312-0044-1).
9. Roger Blanpain, *Women and Labour,* 1978 (ISBN 90-312-0077-8).
10. Roger Blanpain, *European Conference on Labour Law and Industrial Relations: Multinational Enterprises,* 1979 (ISBN 90-312-0091-3).
11. Roger Blanpain, *Job Security and Industrial Relations,* 1980 (ISBN 90-312-0147-2).
12. Roger Blanpain, Greg Bamber & Russell Lansbury, *Technological Change and Industrial Relations: An International Symposium,* 1983 (ISBN 90-312-0205-3).
13. Roger Blanpain, James Janssen van Raay & A. Moulty, *Worker's Participation in the European Community: The Fifth Directive,* 1984 (ISBN 90-654-4187-5).
14. Roger Blanpain, *Equality and Prohibition of Discrimination in Employment,* 1985 (ISBN 90-654-4215-4).
15. Roger Blanpain, *Restructuring Labour in the Enterprise: Law and Practice in France, F.R. of Germany, Italy, Sweden and the United Kingdom,* 1986 (ISBN 90-654-4283-9).
16. Roger Blanpain & E. Kassalow, *Unions and Industrial Relations: Recent Trends and Prospect: A Comparative Treatment,* 1987 (ISBN 90-654-4294-4).
17. Roger Blanpain & Marco Biagi, *Trade Union Democracy and Industrial Relations,* 1988 (ISBN 90-654-4394-0).
18. Roger Blanpain & Jelle Visser, *In Search of Inclusive Unionism,* 1990 (ISBN 90-654-4439-4).
19. Roger Blanpain, *Flexibility and Wages: A Comparative Treatment,* 1990 (ISBN 90-654-4461-0).

20. Roger Blanpain, Stephen Frenkel & Oliver Clarke, *Economic Restructuring and Industrial Relations in Industrialised Countries,* 1990 (ISBN 90-654-4488-2).
21. Roger Blanpain & Friedrich Fürstenberg, *Structure and Strategy in Industrial Relations,* 1991 (ISBN 90-654-4559-5).
22. Roger Blanpain, Amira Galin & Ozer Carmi, *Flexible Work Patterns and Their Impact on Industrial Relations,* 1991 (ISBN 90-654-4572-2).
23. Roger Blanpain, *Workers' Participation: Influence on Management Decision-Making by Labour in the Private Sector,* 1992 (ISBN 90-654-4600-1).
24. Roger Blanpain, Brian Brooks & Chris Engels, *Employed or Self-Employed,* 1992 (ISBN 90-654-4613-3).
25. Roger Blanpain & Tiziano Treu, *Industrial Relations Developments in the Telecommunications Industry,* 1993 (ISBN 90-654-4642-7).
26. Roger Blanpain & Marco Biagi, *Industrial Relations in Small and Medium Sized Enterprises,* 1993 (ISBN 90-654-4696-6).
27. Roger Blanpain & Marco Biagi, *Participative Management and Industrial Relations in a Worldwide Perspective,* 1993 (ISBN 90-654-4769-5).
28. Roger Blanpain, Jacques Rojot & Hoyt N. Wheeler, *Employee Rights and Industrial Justice,* 1994 (ISBN 90-654-4804-7).
29. Roger Blanpain & Ruth Ben-Israel, *Strikes and Lock-Outs in Industrialized Market Economies,* 1994 (ISBN 90-654-4841-1).
30. Roger Blanpain, Kazuo Sugeno & Yasuo Suwa, *The Harmonization of Working Life and Family Life,* 1995 (ISBN 90-411-0064-4).
31. Roger Blanpain & Laszio Nagy, *Labour Law and Industrial Relations in Central and Eastern Europe,* 1996 (ISBN 90-411-0298-1).
32. Roger Blanpain, *Labour Law and Industrial Relations in the European Union,* 1997 (ISBN 90-411-0527-1).
33. Taco Van Peijpe, *Employment Protection under Strain,* 1998 (ISBN 90-411-0528-8).
34. Roger Blanpain, Takashi Araki & Ryuichi Yamakawa, *The Process of Industrialization and the Role of Labour Law in Asia,* 1999 (ISBN 9-041-1104-7-X).
35. Roger Blanpain & Marco Biagi, *Non-standard Work and Industrial Relations,* 1999 (ISBN 90-411-1117-4).
36. Roger Blanpain, *Private Employment Agencies: The Impact of ILO Convention 181 (1997) and the Judgment of the European Court of Justice of 11 December 1997,* 1999 (ISBN 90-411-1118-2).
37. Roger Blanpain, *Multinational Enterprises and the Social Challenges of the XXIst Century: The ILO Declaration on Fundamental* Principles *at Work, Public and Private Corporate Codes of Conduct,* 2000 (ISBN 90-411-1280-4).
38. Roger Blanpain, Ryuichi Yamakawa & Takashi Araki, *Deregulation and Labour Law: In Search of a Labour Concept for the 21st Century,* 2000 (ISBN 90-411-1370-3).
39. Roger Blanpain, *The Council of Europe and the Social Challenges of the XXIst Century,* 2001 (ISBN 90-411-1543-9).

40. Roger Blanpain, *On-Line Rights for Employees in the Information Society, Use & Monitoring of E-Mail & Internet at Work*, 2002 (ISBN 90-411-1626-5).
41. Roger Blanpain, *The Evolving Employment Relationship and the New Economy: The Role of Labour Law & Industrial Relations*, 2001 (ISBN 90-411-1691-5).
42. Roger Blanpain, *Involvement of Employees in the European Union, Works Councils, Company Statute, Information and Consultation Rights*, 2002 (ISBN 90-411-1760-1).
43. Michele Colucci, *The Impact of the Internet and New Technologies on the Workplace: A Legal Analysis from a Comparative Point of View*, 2002 (ISBN 90-411-1824-1).
44. Roger Blanpain, *White Paper on the Labour Market in Italy: The Quality of European Industrial Relations and Changing Industrial Relations*, 2002 (ISBN 90-411-1841-1).
45. Roger Blanpain, Russell D. Lansbury & Young-Bum Park, *Impact of Globalisation on Employment Relations: A Comparison of the Automobile and Banking Industries in Australia and Korea*, 2002 (ISBN 90-411-1850-0).
46. Roger Blanpain & Antoine Jacobs, *Employee Rights in Bankruptcy: A Comparative-Law Assessment*, 2002 (ISBN 90-411-1942-6).
47. Roger Blanpain, Takashi Araki & Shinya Ouchi, *Corporate Restructuring and the Role of Labour Law*, 2003 (ISBN 90-411-1949-3).
48. Roger Blanpain, *Collective Bargaining, Discrimination, Social Security and European Integration*, 2003 (ISBN 90-411-2010-6).
49. Roger Blanpain & Luis Aparicio-Valdez, *Labour Relations in the Asia- Pacific Countries*, 2004 (ISBN 90-411-2239-7).
50. Roger Blanpain & Ronnie Graham, *Temporary Agency Work and the Information Society*, 2004 (ISBN 90-411-2252-4).
51. Roger Blanpain, *The Actors of Collective Bargaining: A World Report*, 2004 (ISBN 90-411-2253-2).
52. Roger Blanpain & Michele Colucci, *The Globalisation of Labour Standards: The Soft Law Track*, 2004 (ISBN 90-411-2303-2).
53. Roger Blanpain, Takashi Araki & Shinya Ouchi, *Labour Law in Motion: Diversification of the Labour Force & Terms and Conditions of Employment*, 2005 (ISBN 90-411-2315-6).
54. Roger Blanpain, *Smoking and the Workplace*, 2005 (ISBN 90-411-2325-3).
55. Roger Blanpain, *Confronting Globalization: The Quest for a Social Agenda*, 2005 (ISBN 90-411-2381-4).
56. Roger Blanpain, Thomas Blanke & Edgar Rose, *Collective Bargaining Wages in Comparative Perspective: Germany, France, the Netherlands, Sweden and the United Kingdom*, 2005 (ISBN 90-411-2388-1).
57. Roger Blanpain & Anne Numhauser-Henning, *Women in Academia & Equality Law: Aiming High - Falling Short?*, 2006 (ISBN 978-90-411-2427-6).
58. Roger Blanpain, *Freedom of Services in the European Union: Labour and Social Security Law: The Bolkestein Initiative*, 2006 (ISBN 978-90-411-2453-5).
59. Roger Blanpain, Frans Pennings & Nurhan Sural, *Flexibilisation and Modernisation of the Turkish Labour Market*, 2006 (ISBN 978-90-411-2490-X).

60. Roger Blanpain & Boel Flodgren, *Corporate and Employment Perspectives in a Global Business Environment*, 2006 (ISBN 978-90-411-2537-X).
61. Roger Blanpain, Shinya Ouchi & Takashi Araki, *Decentralizing Industrial Relations and The Role of Labor Unions and Employee Representatives*, 2007 (ISBN 978-90-411-2583-3).
62. Roger Blanpain, *European Framework Agreements and Telework: Law and Practice: A European and Comparative Study*, 2007 (ISBN 978-90-411-2560-4).
63. Roger Blanpain, Jim Kitay, Leanne Cutcher & Nick Wailes, *Globalization and Employment Relations in Retail Banking*, 2007 (ISBN 978-90-411-2620-1).
64. Roger Blanpain, Russell Lansbury, Jim Kitay, Nick Wailes & Anja Kirsch, *Globalization and Employment Relations in the Auto Assembly Industry: A Study of Seven Countries*, 2008 (ISBN 978-90-411-2698-6).
65. Roger Blanpain & Michele Tiraboschi, *The Global Labour Market: From Globalization to Flexicurity*, 2008 (ISBN 978-90-411-2722-8).
66. Roger Blanpain, Michele Colucci & Frank Hendrickx, *The Future of Sport in the European Union: Beyond the EU Reform Treaty and the White Paper*, 2008 (ISBN 978-90-411-2761-7).
67. Roger Blanpain, Linda Dickens, *Challenges in European Employment Relations: Employment Regulation, Trade Union Organization, Equality, Flexicurity, Training and New Approaches to Pay*, 2008 (ISBN 978-90-411-2771-6).
68. Roger Blanpain, Hiroya Nakakubo & Takashi Araki, *New Developments in Employment Discrimination Law, 2008* (ISBN 978-90-411-2782-2).
69. Roger Blanpain, Andrzej Marian wiątkowski, *The Laval and Viking Cases: Freedom of Services and Establishment v. Industrial Conflict in the European Economic Area and Russia*, 2009 (ISBN 978-90-411-2850-8).
70. Roger Blanpain, William Bromwich, Olga Rymkevich, Silvia Spattini, *The Modernization of Labour Law and Industrial Relations in a Comparative Perspective*, 2009 (ISBN 978-90-411-2865-2).
71. Roger Blanpain, Juan Pablo Landa & Brian Langille, *Employment Policies and Multilevel Governance*, 2009 (ISBN 978-90-411-2866-9).
72. Roger Blanpain, European Works Councils; *The European Directive 2009/ 38/EC of 6 May 2009, 2009* (ISBN 978-90-411-3208-6).
73. Roger Blanpain, William Bromwich, Olga Rymkevich & Silvia Spattini, *Labour Productivity, Investment in Human Capital and Youth Employment: Comparative Developments and Global Responses*, 2010 (ISBN 978-90-411-3249-9).
74. Greg J. Bamber & Philippe Pochet, *Regulating Employment Relations, Work and Labour Laws: International Comparisons between Key Countries*, 2010 (ISBN 978-90-411-3199-7). General Editor: Roger Blanpain.
75. Roger Blanpain, Desislava Nikolaeva Dimitrova, *Seafarers' Rights in the Globalized Maritime Industry*, 2010 (ISBN 978-90-411-3349-6).
76. Roger Blanpain, Hiroya Nakakubo & Takashi Araki, *Regulation of Fixed- Term Employment Contracts*, 2010 (ISBN 978-90-411-3356-4).

77. Roger Blanpain, William Bromwich, Olga Rymkevich & Iacopo Senatori, *Rethinking Corporate Governance*, 2011 (ISBN 978-90-411-3450-9).
78. Roger Blanpain & Frank Hendrickx, *Labour Law between Change and Tradition: Liber Amicorum Antoine Jacobs*, 2011 (ISBN 978-90-411-3424-0).
79. Roger Blanpain, Thomas Klebe, Marlene Schmidt & Bernd Waas, *Trade Union Rights at the Workplace*, 2012 (ISBN 978-90-411-3460-8).
80. Roger Blanpain, William Bromwich, Olga Rymkevich & Iacopo Senatori, *Labour Markets, Industrial Relations and Human Resources Management: From Recession to Recovery*, 2012 (ISBN 978-90-411-4004-3).
81. Roger Blanpain, Hiroya Nakakubo & Takashi Araki, *Systems of Employee Representation at the Enterprise: A Comparative Study*, 2012 (ISBN 978-90-411-4080-7).
82. Roger Blanpain & Frank Hendrickx, *Temporary Agency Work in the European Union and the United States*, 2013 (ISBN 978-90-411-4769-1).
83. Roger Blanpain, Toker Dereli, Y. Pınar Soykut-Sarıca & Aslı en-Tabaı, *Emerging Patterns of Work and Turkish Labour Market Challenges under Globalization: Readings on Labour and Employment Relations*, 2014 (ISBN 978-90-411-4983-1).
84. Roger Blanpain, Pablo Arellano Ortiz, Marius Olivier & Gijsbert Vonk, *Social Security and Migrant Workers: Selected Studies of Cross-border Social Security Mechanisms*, 2014 (ISBN 978-90-411-4770-7).
85. Roger Blanpain & Nikita Lyutov, *Workers' Representation in Central and Eastern Europe: Challenges and Opportunities for the Works Councils' System*, 2014 (ISBN 978-90-411-4746-2).
86. Roger Blanpain, Ulla Liukkunen & Chen Yifeng, *China and ILO Fundamental Principles and Rights at Works*, 2014 (ISBN 978-90-411-4984-8).
87. Roger Blanpain, *The Use of Languages and Employment Relations*, 2014 (ISBN 978-90-411-5606-8).
88. Roger Blanpain, Hiroya Nakakubo & Takashi Araki, *Protection of Employees' Personal Information and Privacy*, 2014 (ISBN 978-90-411-5608-2).
89. Roger Blanpain, Jan Wouters, Glenn Rayp, Laura Beke & Axel Marx, *Protecting Labour Rights in a Multi-polar Supply Chain and Mobile Global Economy*, 2015 (ISBN 978-90-411-5662-4).
90. Roger Blanpain & Stefania Marassi, *Globalization and Transnational Collective Labour Relations: International and European Framework Agreements at Company Level*, 2015 (ISBN 978-90-411-4748-6).
91. Roger Blanpain, Frank Hendrickx & Petra Herzfeld Olsson, *National Effects of the Implementation of EU Directives on Labour Migration from Third Countries*, 2016 (ISBN 978-90-411-6257-1).
92. Roger Blanpain, Frank Hendrickx & D'Arcy du Toit, *Labour Law and Social Progress: Holding the Line or Shifting the Boundaries?* 2016 (ISBN 978-90-411-6747-7).

93. Roger Blanpain & Frank Hendrickx, *Reasonable Accommodation in the Modern Workplace: Potential and Limits of the Integrative Logics of Labour Law*, 2016 (ISBN 978-90-411-6258-8).
94. Roger Blanpain, Frank Hendrickx & Bernd Waas, *New Forms of Employment in Europe*, 2016 (ISBN 978-90-411-6239-7).
95. Roger Blanpain, Frank Hendrickx, Hiroya Nakakubo & Takashi Araki, *The Notion of Employer in the Era of the Fissured Workplace: Should Labour Law Responsibilities Exceed the Boundary of the Legal Entity?*, 2017 (ISBN 978-90-411-8470-2).
96. Elena Sychenko, *Individual Labour Rights as Human Rights: The Contributions of the European Court of Human Rights to Worker's Rights Protection*, 2017 (ISBN 978-90-411-8629-4).
97. William Bromwich & Olga Rymkevich, *Improving Workplace Quality: New Perspectives and Challenges for Worker Well-Being*, 2017 (ISBN 978-90-411-8628-7).
98. Sarah De Groof, *Work-Life Balance in the Modern Workplace: Interdisciplinary Perspectives from Work-Family Research, Law and Policy*, 2017 (ISBN 978-90-411-8630-0).
99. Sylvaine Laulom, *Collective Bargaining Developments in Times of Crisis*, 2018 (ISBN 978-90-411-8999-8).
100. Frank Hendrickx & Valerio De Stefano, *Game Changers in Labour Law: Shaping the Future of Work*, 2018 (ISBN 978-90-411-9953-9).
101. Ivana Palinkaš, *The Legal and Institutional Framing of Collective Bargaining in CEE Countries: Between Europeanisation and Decentralisation*, 2018 (ISBN 978-90-411-9199-1).
102. Jeremy Waddington, *European Board-Level Employee Representation: National Variations in Influence and Power*, 2018 (ISBN 978-90-411-9202-8).
103. Jan Pichrt & Kristina Koldinská, *Labour Law and Social Protection in a Globalized World: Changing Realities in Selected Areas of Law and Policy*, 2018 (ISBN 978-94-035-0093-5).
104. Matthew W. Finkin, *American Labor and the Law: Dormant, Resurgent, and Emergent Problems*, 2019 (ISBN 978-94-035-0654-8).
105. Giuseppe Casale & Tiziano Treu, *Transformations of Work: Challenges for the Institutions and Social Actors*, 2019 (ISBN 978-94-035-0891-7).
106. Miguel De la Corte-Rodríguez, *EU Law on Maternity and Other Child-Related Leaves: Impact on Gender Equality*, 2019 (ISBN 978-94-035-1452-9).
107. Valeria Pulignano & Frank Hendrickx, *Employment Relations in the 21st Century: Challenges for Theory and Research in a Changing World of Work*, 2020 (ISBN 978-94-035-1764-3).
108. Matteo Bottero, *Posting of Workers in EU Law: Challenges of Equality, Solidarity and Fair Competition*, 2021 (ISBN 978-94-035-2860-1).
109. Bernd Waas & Christina Hießl, *Collective Bargaining for Self-Employed Workers in Europe: Approaches to Reconcile Competition Law and Labour Rights*, 2021 (ISBN 978-94-035-2373-6).

110. Mathias Wouters, *International Labour Standards and Platform Work: An Analysis of Digital Labour Platforms Based on the Instruments on Private Employment Agencies, Home Work and Domestic Work*, 2022 (ISBN 978-94-035-4024-5).
111. Luca Ratti, *In-Work Poverty in Europe: Vulnerable and Under-Represented Persons in a Comparative Perspective*, 2022 (ISBN 978-94-035-4996-5).
112. Silvia Rainone, *The Role of the Court of Justice in EU Labour Law: A Case Study on the Transfer of Undertakings Directive*, 2023 (ISBN 978-94-035-2896-0).
113. Frank Hendrickx, Elena Gramano & David Mangan, *Privacy@work: A European and Comparative Perspective*, 2023 (ISBN 978-94-035-3106-9).
114. Elena Sychenko & Adalberto Perulli, *Employment Law and the European Convention on Human Rights: The Research of the Recent Jurisprudence of the ECtHR Related to Employment Law (2017-2021)*, 2023 (ISBN 978-94-035-3556-2).

Made in United States
North Haven, CT
04 November 2026

21727468R00085